After the Electronic Revolution, Will You Be the First to Go?

PROCEEDINGS OF THE 1992
ASSOCIATION FOR LIBRARY COLLECTIONS & TECHNICAL SERVICES
PRESIDENT'S PROGRAM • 29 JUNE 1992
AMERICAN LIBRARY ASSOCIATION ANNUAL CONFERENCE
SAN FRANCISCO, CA

Arnold Hirshon
Editor

American Library Association
Chicago and London 1993

Project editor: Bruce Frausto

Cover designed by Harriet Banner

Composed by ALA Production Services in Garamond
and Avant-Garde using Ventura Publisher 3.0

Printed on 50-pound Finch Opague, a pH-neutral stock,
and bound in 10-pt. C1S cover stock by IPC, St. Joseph, Michigan

The paper used in this publication meets the minumum
requirements of the American National Standard for Information
Sciences—Permanence of Paper for Printed Library Materials,
ANSI Z39.48-1984.

ISBN 0-8389-7650-6

TP

Contents

Preface

Arnold Hirshon

Libraries are failing because they are tied inexorably to the past. They are failing because they are a design of the conventional wisdom and so reinforce their values and their stale ritual without question, without remorse. They fail because they are morally and psychologically bound to the physical plan and to the physical objects, rather than to clients and to problem solving. . . . It is very difficult, it may be impossible, for a conventional, passive, and complacent professional discipline to break dramatically with the past. Yet, precisely this is necessary if librarianship is to survive as anything other than a custodial function.—Paul Wasserman, *The New Librarianship: A Challenge for Change* (1972)[1]

In the revolutionary 1960s, when those of us in my generation thought we would change the world by growing long hair and wearing bell-bottom pants, our most pressing concern was what would happen after (not if) we took control. We would shake up the traditional order, replace the old with the new, and decide such weighty issues as who would be the first to go "after the revolution." Well the 1960s are past, but within librarianship the changes brought about by electronic information are causing a new revolution, a new paradigm shift. If Wasserman's comments were prescient twenty years ago, then today we are truly living on borrowed time. We are no longer wondering about whom we will overthrow; instead, our profession in its middle age must look over its shoulder and wonder whether the advent of the electronic revolution will mean that *we* will be the first to go.

The idea for this President's Program was inspired by the pioneering work of those who have spoken and written about paradigm shifts, such as Thomas Kuhn and Joel Barker. Kuhn spoke about paradigm shifts in the scientific community,[2] and Barker has applied those observations to the world of management. Noting that paradigms are the rules for our current ways of doing things, Barker recognizes that these rules and processes help to bring order to our lives. But the rules also blind us to some possible new ways of doing things—the "we've always done it this way" trap. When we are faced with a new idea, Barker observes that we rarely accept it on its own terms, but, rather, we try to understand it through our old, and outmoded, paradigms.[3]

The problem is that when the change is occurring, we are least likely to recognize its importance. We are so close to the problem that we do not have a proper perspective. I was reminded of this in a small way when reading an article about Judy Garland and the making of the *Wizard of Oz*. The article noted that

> The Wizard of Oz is timeless . . . yet M-G-M obviously had no idea that the film was to become a classic—the studio had so little inkling of what was classic about it that its all-embracing anthem, "Over the Rainbow," was very nearly dropped at the last minute; it was thought to be slowing up the action.[4]

Perhaps most important, Barker instructs us that when a paradigm shifts, our past success will guarantee nothing. He states succinctly "When the shift occurs, everyone goes back to zero." In other words, libraries and librarians may have been around for a few thousand years, but with the paradigm shift of the electronic revolution there is no guarantee that we will be around as a profession in the future. As Paul Wasserman wrote in 1972, "The fact that libraries have survived as long as they have in their present condition and with their present commitments makes them no less vulnerable."[5]

These proceedings should challenge you to be one of the electronic revolutionaries. The 1992 ALCTS President's Program was the first of two President's Programs to address the effects of electronic publishing on libraries. The second program will occur at the 1993 ALA Annual Conference. The 1992 program included a distinguished panel of individuals whose role was not to provide answers, but rather to raise questions about where information access is going both outside of librarianship and within it. It is up to you, the reader, to decide where you will fit in that picture.

Each of the speakers brought a special perspective to the proceedings, and a selected passage from each of their papers gives only a hint of the intellectual challenges presented in these proceedings.

In "The Convergence of Publishing and Bibliographic Access," I set forth a general premise that the information that users are seeking and the access mechanisms are moving from a two-stage process to become one:

> Electronic information is likely to bring with it some basic paradigm shifts that will inexorably change the course of both the dissemination of, and access to, information. First, electronic information has a detached phys-

icality, existing "virtually" but not "physically" in the same sense that the book has had as a physical object. Second, printed information has always been fixed and static; once packaged between a set of covers, information changed only with the issuance of a new edition. Electronic information has the potential to always be in a dynamic state. Of course any form of communication has some degree of stasis, but clearly electronic information is more dynamic than its predecessors.

Ted Nelson, the keynote speaker, addresses the changes in electronic communication that we can expect in the outside information world:

> *You cannot tell the future what to become.* You can adapt to it and you can see where it's going. If you understand it correctly and understand its continuity with the past, and how to make it all fit with the major ideas of the past, perhaps everything will work out. I say this because while many groups I speak to consider me the most raving radical they have ever heard, I consider myself to be a deep traditionalist. I merely transpose what I consider to be the most important ideas of Western civilization to their obvious next form. To be misled by the superficial appearance of this transposed form and to fail to see its historical essence—what it carries over from the past—is to miss the whole point.

> There is a great system of which you librarians have been the traditional guardians (and I speak with the greatest affection and respect for your profession and hope that we can find some reasonable new form for it). That great system is called *literature.* We don't think of it as a system, any more than the fish thinks of the water as a system, but it is. Literature is a system whereby *millions of ideas run on compatible equipment.* These pieces of compatible equipment are called *desks, shelves,* and *minds.* We can put a book, a magazine, and a pamphlet that someone has preserved from the seventeenth century all on the same desk and compare them, and lo! They are all running on the same equipment without installation. . . .

> Now we turn to the biggest question: *Why provide service by the fragment?* Why buy separate pieces rather than the whole document? One reason is that you may not want the whole document at a given time. The second reason (and this is the important part because it cleans up nearly 90 percent of the copyright issue) is that it means that *any author can quote any other author in this great repository without permission.* Why? Because the quotation is *not a copy* as it is in the print system. In the electronic system, the quotation is a *pointer.* The quote or illustration is a *transclusion pointer* that sends a message to the user's screen that says "Go buy that illustration from the original." So quoted the material is bought from the original publisher at the moment of request, with automatic royalty to the original publisher with automatic credit to the original author. These things are automatically sorted out. Plagiarism (except for a few people who don't understand the system and behave inanely . . .) is a thing of the past, and credit is utterly clear.

Peter Graham addresses the technical services perspective of libraries and speaks particularly to the preservation of electronic information:

> The problem may be put in the form of several questions that confront the user of any electronic document (whether it is text, graphic, numeric, or multimedia information) because the problems are similar. How can I be sure that what I am reading is what I wanted to read? . . . How can a reader be sure that the document being used is the one intended?
>
> We properly take for granted the fixity of text in the print world: The printed journal article I examine because of the footnote you gave is beyond question the same text that you read. Therefore we have confidence that our discussion is based upon a common foundation. The present state of electronic texts is such that we no longer can have that confidence.

Susan Martin presents the administrator's and library public services' perspective, and she sets forth a vision of what will be needed for librarians to succeed in the future:

> The leadership category is intended to suggest the need for librarians to be proactive. If librarianship is to take responsibility for molding the information environment and ensuring that individuals receive the information they need to make knowledgeable decisions, we must be recognized as a force, a power that carries with it the weight of experience, expertise, and reasonableness. To that end, the visions statement suggests that we take steps to reinforce and emphasize our leadership role, which is now minimal or nonexistent. This is a courageous step; it will require boldness and some risk taking. Since we're not known for an excessive amount of either characteristic, the world will be surprised.

Thomas Duncan writes from the perspective of an informed user, discussing how university faculty must be a part of altering their accustomed systems to develop a new structure for using electronic information:

> To build an information technology infrastructure, academics at universities have a responsibility to participate in and foster the development of scholarly electronic information systems, foster collaboration with colleagues, and develop explicit practices that encourage sharing of data. These efforts can significantly enhance the building of and contribution to disciplinewide factual and reference databases.
>
> In addition, faculty should simultaneously begin the reevaluation of traditional notions of research; traditional measures of scholarly activities; training of students who wish to enter the academy; and dissemination of academic work to satisfy a broader audience.
>
> The changes that such reevaluation portends are as much a revolution within the academy as the building of the information technology infrastructure required to participate effectively in future research, teaching, and public service. The development of an effective information technology infrastructure and its impact will require serious attention by faculty.

So sit back, explore the future, and decide for yourself: After the electronic revolution, will you be the first to go?

Notes

1. Paul Wasserman, *The New Librarianship: A Challenge for Change* (New York: Bowker, 1972), xi.

2. Thomas S. Kuhn, *The Structure of Scientific Revolutions* (Chicago: University of Chicago, 1962).

3. Joel A. Barker, *Discovering the Future: The Business of Paradigms* (Burnsville, MN: Charthouse, 1989), videocassette. See also his *Future Edge: Discovering the New Paradigms of Success* (New York: Morrow, 1992).

4. Ethan Mordden, "A Critic at Large: I Got a Song," *The New Yorker*, Oct. 22, 1990, 120.

5. Wasserman, 1972, 5.

The Convergence of Publishing and Bibliographic Access

Arnold Hirshon

Is Information *Becoming* Access?

Let us start with two elemental observations:

- Since the invention of the printing press, there has been no change so fundamental to the publishing industry as the advent of electronic and networked information.
- Since the invention of the card catalog, no innovation has so profoundly transformed libraries as the advent of the electronic index, electronic abstract, and the electronic catalog.

The point of these two remarks might be superficially obvious. The application of electronic technology has had a profound effect on both publishing and on libraries. What is less obvious is an implied third statement nesting between the two. In the past, the traditional methods for distributing information (in the form of printed publications) and for accessing information (the library catalog and series of indexes) were separate. Each development pursued a separate course. Upon the action of the publisher to disseminate *information*, libraries reacted by creating separate but related access mechanisms for bibliographic *access.*

And so not always by design and not always in strict fashion, the histories of publishing and librarianship have been two parallel time lines, two continua, that traveled through time independently with occasional crossovers. Throughout our mutual histories the publisher's actions and library's reactions were generally complementary but distinct. Access to information was a two-step process, physically represented between the presence of the book on the shelf and the library catalog to help find that book.

Paradigm Shifting into Electronic Overdrive

Electronic information is likely to bring with it some basic paradigm shifts that will inexorably change the course of both the dissemination of, and access to, information. First, electronic information has a detached physicality, existing "virtually" but not "physically" in the same sense that the book has had as a physical object. Second, printed information has always been fixed and static; once packaged between a set of covers, information changed only with the issuance of a new edition. Electronic information has the potential to always be in a dynamic state. Of course any form of communication has some degree of stasis, but clearly electronic information is more dynamic than its predecessors.

Another fundamental change brought by the advent of electronic and networked information is that it blurs the lines between the mechanisms for accessing and for retrieving information. In today's world, "publishing" is moving toward "information distribution." Similarly, libraries have been moving from "bibliographic" management to "information" management. Books once required a library catalog to organize and retrieve them. For electronic communications on a network, the access mechanism and the retrieval are becoming virtually one, and our historic publishing and bibliographic access continua may well be on a path also to becoming one.

Planning for the Electronic Revolution

We have the advantage today of being able to see this change coming and to be able to adjust to it. This is an evolutionary change that will likely have revolutionary implications. This convergence of publishing and access will make it imperative that libraries employ strategic planning. Through proper application of strategic management, libraries can look at the external publishing environment and relate our internal organizations to that environment. By doing so, we in libraries can maximize our strengths and limit our weaknesses.

The first step is to recognize when and how the change is likely to occur. In this regard, there are at least four factors that affect the nature and pace of widespread change in libraries:

1. *Users must want the change, not just need it.* Most people must have a pressing reason to change old habits. Simply having a good product

is not sufficient reason. In the case of libraries, it is the library users who must express their need for the change.

2. *Technology must be fully mature, not just available.* For example, the technology to provide automated indexes in the library was available many years before we started to use it. Only the medium of delivery, CD-ROM, was different. This difference in technology, however, was sufficient to delay more widespread use.

3. *The cost must be low, not just affordable.* Libraries are not wealthy, and the publishing industry is not as lucrative as librarians tend to imagine. Compared with other American industries, publishers run on a small profit margin. Therefore, if technology is to grab hold, it must be affordable for both publishers and libraries.

4. *The system must be intuitively easy to use.* The best system in the world will have limited application if only a limited number of people can figure out how to use it. This helps explain why so many people today use microcomputers, but so few people had used mainframes.

Are all of these conditions applicable today? Probably not. Librarians may be ahead of some of the users in perceiving the inevitability and desirability of electronic information. The technology is not yet fully mature. Much of the electronic information is clumsy, and little nontextual information is available that is inexpensive or available for rapid delivery. However, these current factors should be seen not as limitations, but rather as opportunities. We are being given a few precious years (and probably our last opportunity) to make the transition to master this new form of communication, to make it our own, and to present ourselves as the natural teachers and navigators.

Already we are seeing different types of electronic publications, and some trends are beginning to solidify. Paul Starr makes a powerful case for electronic communication. He also notes that there are likely to be at least three forms of publications: on-demand publishing, which will reduce the manufacturing costs; online publishing, including the current database services and electronic journals; and electronic editions of texts, which can be read on a personal computer and incorporate interactive routines, graphics, and sound.[1] Each of these forms of communication will place differing demands upon libraries for service and differing demands upon librarians to have the abilities and skills to provide those services.

One part of the equation is likely to remain the same. Publishers will continue to play the active part, with librarians as the reactors. Publishers will move to change the principles under which copyright royalties are assessed, and librarians will be forced to rethink the paradigms under which we developed our old rules and regulations for copyright. We should not see this as a threat, because each of us has a rightful niche. The question is whether we as librarians will seize the opportunity to redefine the precepts of our profession in light of a new paradigm.

Where Are We Today?

I first posited the idea in 1989 that the electronic revolution was moving libraries and publishers toward a merging of our parallel continua. In the intervening years, there has been clear progress in having access and information become a one-step process. Nowhere is this more visible than with direct free-text-search access to the database of information. The development of systems on the Internet, such as WAIS, Gopher, and Archie—client/server systems—are the incipient forms of the combining of information and access. These systems may be clumsy, but so were the first online catalogs. The changes in information technology are likely to accelerate this scenario.

Over the last few years our profession seems to have moved toward a common if not conventional wisdom about the future, including some of the following beliefs:

- Information in the future will increasingly be electronic.
- Electronic information will be distributed rather than centralized.
- Access will be increasingly direct rather than through secondary systems.
- Access to information will replace ownership of information, and on-demand provision of information will replace on-the-shelf subscriptions and books.

If these visions are correct, what are the implications for our profession? Libraries as organizations traditionally have been more internally driven than externally driven. Rather than mold ourselves to the habits of the users or the vagaries of publishing, we have often done what was best for ourselves. A classic example was our adoption of microforms. Microforms were to librarianship what liver was to nutrition: We didn't like either one, but we thought it was supposed to be good for you. Today we know that microforms never became as dominant as once predicted for the same reason that liver is no longer popular: Not only didn't we like them, but they weren't very good for us either. The nutritional value of liver can be better found in other foods that are lower in cholesterol, while the user can find information in better formats than microforms. Microforms simply did not have enough added value to outweigh their liabilities. The primary beneficiaries of microforms were libraries, not patrons. Libraries gained space, and users got eyestrain. By contrast, electronic communication brings an added value for both libraries and users, because retrieval is more rapid and the information is delivered in a format that is amenable to ready manipulation.

Because of the dynamic nature of electronic communications, we must begin to undertake a fundamental rethinking of librarianship. Rather than continuing to control flat and nondynamic data through the application of precoordinated control of information (that is, our traditional library catalog), libraries must provide information in the way that the user wants it through free-text access accessible through hypertext.

Not only must our systems change, but so must our data. We must question whether the databases we are building and maintaining are about to become irrelevant dinosaurs. If we are to survive, we must begin working on new retrieval methods other than the MARC format. As networked information systems provide not only the information but also the access mechanisms, coded text, in the form of the Standard Generalized Markup Language (SGML), will become more prevalent.[2] The primary benefit of SGML is that it provides a way to identify and tag the parts of the full text of an electronic manuscript, so computers can easily differentiate the parts. Once the full text is tagged, it is quite possible that the next level of electronic information delivery systems will be able to move us away from the secondary level of access that the MARC format was intended to provide. As our old systems give way to new ones, will we continue to limp along without fundamentally thinking about what we are doing or why?

Rather than continuing to expend our resources to convert our current bibliographic records, one strategic approach would be for libraries to band together in a concerted effort to convert printed works into definitive versions of electronic texts, not only for the preservation aspects but to expand access. As technical services librarians, we should also be concerned with what is happening with the archives of electronic works created by commercial and noncommercial publishers. Have publishers been retaining their computer archives, or have they simply been dumping them or keeping them in nonrefreshed files? Unfortunately, publishers are only beginning to become aware of the capital investment that they have in their computer files. Too often publishers still see electronic data as a means to produce a print product and not as a valuable end product in and of itself. Strategic partnerships between publishers and librarians to preserve the original electronic manuscripts could well lead to some important roles for libraries in the future.

The result of changes wrought in the electronic world will be a radical transformation in the historic continua of publishing and bibliographic access. As information and the method of access become one, the two parallel lines increasingly show signs of blurring and converging. Libraries may become more interested in the creation of (not merely access to) information, and publishers may find that they can provide both the access and information in a single package. And as new forms of communication lead to new approaches to bibliographic information, this should in turn lead to new organizational structures for libraries. By strategically developing our services within the larger world of scholarly communication, we can realize significant organizational change during the next twenty-five years.

In the 1970s, with the advent of OCLC, technical services grabbed all of the technological attention in libraries. In the 1980s, with online indexes and CD-ROMs, the attention shifted to library public services. Somewhere along the way we forgot that the true battleground was not within our walls, but outside them. In the 1990s and the twenty-first century, with access instead of ownership becoming a reality, and information access becoming less place-bound, the question is not whether public or technical services will grab the technological attention, but rather whether the library will have *any* place in providing information. In short, we need to question what role there will be for librarians in selecting, acquiring, cataloging, or preserving information in the nontraditional world we face. For example, should we worry less about the increasing cost of print journal subscriptions and more about the economics of *electronic* information?

The Challenges of the Present Will Form the Basis of Our Future

The electronic revolution clearly is a paradigm shift. Michael Malinconico in his May 1, 1992, article in *Library Journal* challenges us and says that thus far

> we have constructed scenarios of the emerging electronic library [that] assume the continuity of present institutional and organizational structures. The most popular of these [scenarios] assumes that the institutions currently identified as libraries will increasingly acquire modern technology.

Malinconico goes on to state:

> Regrettably, we have failed to consider another equally plausible scenario whereby information resources are drawn into the orbits of influence of those who maintain the technological infrastructures. . . . We have not examined critically the consequences of this possibility despite evidence suggesting that this scenario may be the most plausible.[3]

The electronic revolution has the potential to have profound effects on our libraries and on technical services operations. This is a time when we ought to be questioning ourselves and challenging the profession. For example:

- As information and access become one, will libraries be forced to develop new ways to allocate budgets and new measures of library service?

- How will the adaptation to the world of electronic communication change the demand for different skills and abilities from library professionals?
- Should libraries move from being passive information users to information providers? Should libraries begin to encourage the development of electronic texts?
- As we move away from local generation of our catalogs to direct use of the text to generate indexes, will the individual library technical services operation and technical services librarian become an anachronism?

Visions and Focus

If we are smart, we will begin immediately to redefine our role. If information and access are converging into one, will there continue to be a need for librarians to maintain the databases and establish retrieval protocols? Will there be a need to manage a collection when the entire collection is a virtual one? Will we have a role to play in setting standards for information creation and maintenance?

In modern librarianship there have been three major visions related to text retrieval. The first, in 1876, was Cutter's Principles of the Catalog. The second occurred largely during the late 1960s and early 1970s, when visionaries in our profession set forth goals to integrate all functions within a single library system and have all the functions operating from a unified master data record. Although we had hoped to have these automated systems available by the mid-1970s, we know now that they did not predominate in libraries until the 1990s.

What library collections and technical services managers need today is a new guiding vision. We must tie our vision for librarianship to the future of electronic communication. Just as we are now trying to integrate external information sources, such as reference databases, into our own library catalog database, soon we will witness a complete bibliographic upheaval. The integration this time will be complete because we will finally get the scholar directly from the keyword to the text, rather than through the many subsidiary steps the scholar must now take. It may have taken twenty years to achieve our first vision of the online catalog, and it may be that long before we achieve our second.

Even more important than setting forth a vision is to begin to focus on how we will develop and maintain organizational adaptation mechanisms. Rather than wait until finality is thrust upon us, we should begin this work today. For only if we continually evaluate and adapt to the evolutionary changes will our future take care of itself. If we fail to meet the challenges, the future will take care of us.

Notes

1. Paul Starr, "The Electronic Reader," *Daedalus 112*, no. 1 (1983): 143–46.

2. National Information Standards Organization (Z39), American National Standard for Information Sciences, *Electronic Manuscript Preparation and Markup (Standard Z39.59-1986)* (Washington: National Information Standards Organization, 1986).

3. S. Michael Malinconico, "Information's Brave New World," *Library Journal* 17, no.8 (May 1, 1992): 36–40.

You, the Guardians of Literature Still

Theodor Holm Nelson
Keynote Speaker

You Cannot Tell the Future
What to Become

About 1932, people thought that by now we would have robots ironing our shirts. Instead, they invented permanent press! This is a deep insight: *Things don't necessarily come in the package that fits the old model.* Similarly, the earliest horseless carriages had sockets for a buggy whip. This was felt to be comforting. I am not sure at whom they would crack the whip, but somehow this continuity made the new vehicle more comfortable. In the nineteenth century we had an army and we had a navy, and so the natural question when aircraft were invented was: "Well, what are they? Are they ships, or are they brigades?" And the answer is they were airplanes, and they eventually went under a new command. These are examples to adjust your frame of mind: *The invention is rarely to your specifications.*

Xerox has had a very paradoxical history. In 1937, I believe—the year I was born—a man named Chester Carlson invented the principle of a new copying machine. I read about this when I was thirteen years old; how there was going to be a machine that would allow you to make copies for a nickel each. And by the time I was fifteen I thought, "Gee whiz, I would really like to have a lot of copies," because I was already deeply involved in manuscripts and multiple versions in my own writings. In the fall of 1953 I actually made a number of calls throughout Manhattan trying to find out where to get the services of the new copier from the Haloid Corporation, which supposedly offered this new copying machine. I was very disappointed to find out that all the copy companies that advertised in the yellow pages responded "No, no, copies cost two bucks each!" It wasn't until ten years later that the Haloid Corporation changed its name to Xerox and brought out its first copying machine, furnishing the low-cost copies Carlson intended.

Part one of the Xerox story, then, was the wonderful and accurate faith of the Haloid Corporation. For some fifteen years they continued to put fifty thousand dollars a year into the development of this process that no one else thought had any potential, until at last they were able to bring out their new copying technology, which revolutionized the world of paper. Carlson and Haloid saw in advance the change that would come.

But part two of this story is ironic and paradoxical. Xerox proceeded to fund a large segment of computer research, at the cutting edge and the frontier, and they created prototypes. Because they could no longer imagine the future, they threw it away. The so-called Macintosh actually began as the Alto at Xerox Palo Alto Research Center in 1970. Xerox, by then an absolutely committed paper company, kept pouring in millions of dollars and saying, "No, no, no, you've got the wrong idea. What we want is tomorrow's systems of *paper!*" The guys at Palo Alto kept saying, "You don't get it. Screens are what are going to happen, so we are working on the best possible screens." Xerox kept saying "No, no, no, no, no! You don't understand. The mandate is it will be PAPER!" And the guys in the back room said, "No, the fact is, it won't!"

The result finally was that Xerox was unable to bring out a successful product using any of these computer-screen ideas, and others took over. Steven Jobs of Apple walked through and said, "Oh, that's a good idea." And he brought out first a computer called the Lisa, and then a computer called the Macintosh, which finally caught on. And of course now Apple claims all of the credit for the windows and icons that Xerox Palo Alto Research Center developed. Here is the moral: Young Xerox saw a new box for the future, and then the old Xerox thought they could make the future fit into what was now its old box.

Now, I think you get the drift of what I am saying. *You cannot tell the future what to become.* You can adapt to it and you can see where it's going. If you understand it correctly and understand its continuity with the past, and how to make it all fit with the major ideas of the past, perhaps everything will work out. I say this because while many groups I speak to consider me the most raving radical they have ever heard, I consider myself to be a deep traditionalist. I merely transpose what I consider to be the most important ideas of Western civilization to their obvious next form. To be misled by the superficial appearance of this transposed form and to fail to see its historical essence—what it carries over from the past—is to miss the whole point.

But of course in different eras we hear different things. As the editor of *Creative Computing* magazine, I once mistakenly published an article that some poor fool had plagiarized from the *Scientific American* and gave us permission to publish. That was the end of his academic career. But I am deeply embarrassed because I had actually read the article in the *Scientific American*, and it had seemed to me murky, obscure, and badly written. When I read it several years later in a relatively obscure British journal under a new authorship, I said: "Gee, this is extremely clear and well done." This was because, of course, my own understanding of the subject had changed and the document (being newly typeset and differently illustrated) appeared to me to be a completely different object. So I am embarrassed also by the fact that my own perception was less clear than I wish it had been. But this is something we all do. We hear different things at different times. We read the same book, and it is a different book at the different times that we read it.

A Monstrous and Twisted Caricature

So the ideas that I am going to tell you now are what I have been working on for thirty-two years without a break, in identical form. I haven't changed my paradigm in thirty-two years, because I already changed it rather early. People who heard me speak twenty years ago, or twenty-five years ago, come up to me and say, "Golly, Ted, everything that you have said has come to pass!" I say: "No, no, a thousand times no!" What we have today is a monstrous and twisted caricature of what it must become. The so-called computer literacy is a hideous tangle of nonsensical details with which no one should have to bother. A few computer guys decided back in 1947 (when there were fewer than fifty computer guys in the world) to store files with short names in hierarchical directories. Newcomers to the computer field are now told that this is the God-given way that computers are meant to hold information.

I find this highly obnoxious and totally contrary to any reasonable interconnection of thoughts, a parody of the structure of information. Yet it is our fossilized view that this is the way computers *work*. In fact, the way computers work is a simple selection of arbitrary choices that have been made in different years and different places by different people with different schemes and motivations, all arching into an idiotic conglomerate that we somehow take as divinely ordained.

New divine myths continue to appear. A Mr. Bill Gates, in the Seattle area, defining the world for his own interest, has persuaded us that electronic publishing is the issuance of things called CD-ROMs. How someone can think that selling plastic is electronic publishing, I don't know. But he has millions of people fooled in this regard!

The System of Literature

So the question is: Where are we going? Or, more properly, How may our divine intelligences divert this computer juggernaut from its inane trajectory?

Let's go back to first principles. We have a much older system, a very great and wonderful system with which nearly everyone in the world is familiar. We don't see it as a system any more than, supposedly, fish see the water. (They say that fish don't see the water, but I have seen fish jump out of the water. Fish must be aware that they are in or out of something or other. So too may we figure out what *we* are in.)

There is a great system of which you librarians have been the traditional guardians (and I speak with the greatest affection and respect for your profession and hope that we can find some reasonable new form for it). That great system is called *literature*. We don't think of it as a system, any more than the fish thinks of the water as a system, but it is. Literature is a system whereby *millions of ideas run on compatible equipment.* These pieces of compatible equipment are called *desks, shelves*, and *minds.* We can put a book, a magazine, and a pamphlet that someone has preserved from the seventeenth century all on the same desk and compare them, and lo! They are all running on the same equipment without installation.

A deeper aspect of this system is that it is very well *debugged.* What it allows is the intercomparison, commingling, and working together of all the ideas and points of view that have been placed for our use on these pieces of paper.

It is an accident that paper is the present medium. Once it was parchment, once it was clay. Some of you may actually have custodianship of objects of parchment or even clay that are part of this system of literature. As, no doubt, you have custodianship of CD-ROMs, which are even in their uniquely clumsy way also a part of this literature.

What I am leading to is the idea that literature as a system will continue and prevail. What will continue is that *different points of view, from different minds, registered for preservation and transmission in various forms of words and pictures and diagrams, will move from mind to surface to eye to mind.* The surface may change and indeed is changing. As we had clay, as we had parchment, as we have paper, so the next surface is the glowing screen. No particular type of screen has any preeminent destiny. Technologies of screens are changing constantly. Projection screens may come and go: liquid crystal, cathode-ray tubes, whatever. In ten or fifteen years someone may actually develop the three-dimensional display device (sometimes called a tank in science fiction) that allows the image to coruscate in the room in front of you like the image of the Princess Laia in *Star Wars*, brought by R2D2 as the custodian. The form of the screen, the form of the presentation, are matters of indifference, just as the hue of the paper, the weight of the paper, and whether the book is in octavo or quarto format are matters of indifference to the content in the world of paper.

The particulars of the presentational mechanism cannot be intrinsic to the document. What is a *document?* It is that capsule (or, as computer people say, "encapsulation") of the words, the thoughts, the ideas that are being saved and presented to the user. The document is going to have words, and it is going to have pictures.

Databases as the Alternative to Literature

What is the alternative to literature? The alternative is the view that the technoids are trying to hand you. ("Technoid" is another term I coined that seems to be popular these days.) The technoids are trying to hand you the *database*. Now there is nothing wrong with a database, just as there is nothing wrong with file cards, because a database is nothing but a bunch of virtual file cards. But the technoids say we won't have documents anymore, and we won't have writing. All we will have are databases. To them, I reply, "Wrong!" A database is really a document because it contains a point of view.

Points of view are at the heart of the literary system. I see this system of ongoing documents and literature as a parade. I remember parades when I was a kid in New York, where people would carry lots of placards. Literature is like a parade. The placards represent a point of view, much as a document expresses the ideas of the person who carries it. Literature is this great parade that has lasted for thousands of years and may last many thousands more. As points of view march forward, people yell at us trying to get our attention and try to make us see the truth as they believe it to be.

The database notion, by contrast, is the view that the universe is just a system of *facts*, and documents are facts connected by goo, by sentences that aren't really necessary. Nuance, innuendo, connotation, implication— all these things are irrelevant to the database point of view because when we have just the facts ("Just the facts, ma'am, just the facts," said Sergeant Friday) we won't need all those ideas anymore.

The connective tissue of the universe is ideas. Facts, whatever they may be, are far less certain than the technoids would have us imagine. Every database is really a shoe box of *alleged* facts, as alleged by the promoter and maintainer of that database. This can be very useful if the data are about something simple with well-defined boundaries, such as data concerning airplane crashes, countries of the world, or major corporations. The database may have a certain degree of accuracy for that moment in time with regard to its particular screening mechanism, the circumstances under which those factoids were collected, ruled out, welcomed in. But all of these hidden screening mechanisms are not acknowledged by the database people.

A database has a *point of view*, just as much as a poem does. A database also becomes a *document* in the great march of literature.

What literature is and will remain is a great parade, a system of connected documents. Every library has a sampling from this great parade in the form of paper documents with points of view. This system of paper representation and storage and presentation has served us extremely well.

The last thing I want to do is see any of these books lost. People accuse me of not loving books. On the contrary, I love books *too much!* I have storerooms full of books! I have more books than anyone I know, and *I can't find them.* I merely want instantaneous access to all these writings and pictures and words without having to go and blow the dust off a carton and open it up and get rid of the insects that are in the carton or whatever happens to be the circumstances that hide that particular book or magazine. The documents should all be right there on your screen.

Toward a New System of Publishing and Royalties

What is the next step? It seems to me obvious that the next step is electronic storage and transmission. However, in a system that retains the necessary literary structure of documents and points of view, the new system may be quite different from what you may be hearing from some people. We will retain the integrity of the document that the author or authors who created it intended.

We will still have the necessity of maintaining that object and its integrity. But we will have an additional opportunity: the opportunity to maintain the document's connections to everything else. The new form of publishing I foresee (and this was the vision that I had in October of 1960) is that we will not only have a repository network for the instantaneous availability of all documents to all screens, but this system will carry automatic royalty and allow for multiple users of the same material.

Let us stop here, because to some people the idea of electronic delivery *with royalties* is already so shocking, so astounding, that they can't get past it. Let's get past it. The point is that we have a world in which an economic basis makes sense. We have just discovered in the collapse of the Soviet Union that a world without a sensible economic basis falls apart. The two commodities—money and prestige—have been the right and left hands of motivation in the literary world. An economic basis that makes sense for publishers means that both publishers and authors will continue to be motivated in appropriate ways, by the same money and prestige that have always motivated them.

While the system requires automatic royalty on what is delivered, payment should be by the piece, not by the document. In other words, you do not call the individual document to your screen, but instead just a fragment at a time. You don't have to buy the whole document, you just pay as you go, buy the first three paragraphs, or the tenth illustration. An automatic royalty payment goes from your account to the publisher's account.

Now obviously you have to know the cost of the royalty in advance so you can approve the charge. And the royalty has to be small, because (and here is the kicker) if the cost is high, people will exchange data copies illicitly.

The cost of this form of distribution is intrinsically far lower than what we are paying for paper documents now. Built into the cost of a book or magazine are the costs for the printing, the paper, paper delivery, and storage, all those newsstands, and all those beautiful publisher's buildings with air-conditioning, heating, and janitorial service. The manifest destiny of literature is to get the document to the consumer "instantaneously" (currently within a few minutes, later perhaps in seconds).

This is particularly true because we can arrange for the clean archiving of all of the literature out there. This brings up the issue of authentication. When you hold a paper document in your hands you can tell when it was printed, and you can get some sense of its authenticity by the color of the paper, by what has happened to the edges, by the binding, or by the typeface. In the age of the electronic document, all of these ephemeral characteristics are totally gone or easily forged. However, we may thank researchers such as Hellmann and Diffie, Rivest, Shamir, and Adleman for giving us the technology of authentication that will make it possible to know that a document is not a counterfeit. [A further discussion of authentication appears in the chapter by Peter Graham in this book.—*Ed.*]

Now we turn to the biggest question: *Why provide service by the fragment?* Why buy separate pieces rather than the whole document? One reason is that you may not want the whole document at a given time. The second reason (and this is the important part because it cleans up nearly 90 percent of the copyright issue) is that it means that *any author can quote any other author in this great repository without permission.* Why? Because the quotation is *not a copy* as it is in the print system. In the electronic system, the quotation is a *pointer.* The quote or illustration is a *transclusion pointer* that sends a message to the user's screen that says "Go buy that illustration from the original." So quoted the material is bought from the original publisher at the moment of request, with automatic royalty to the original publisher with automatic credit to the original author. These things are automatically sorted out. Plagiarism (except for a few people who don't understand the system and behave inanely, like the guy who copied the article out of the *Scientific American*) is a thing of the past, and credit is utterly clear.

Those are the economics of the publishing system. What is going to make this new system run is the fact that the small publishers will jump on it. The big publishers won't come near it for a long time. They know too much. They are too smart. McGraw-Hill has perhaps ten different computer departments and projects. What could they possibly want with such a system? But the little publishers see a new revenue stream with no effort. They already have a book on disk. For a ten-to-fifty dollar deposit they have a book published electronically throughout the world. What will drive the system will be the thrust of a million people who have computers and who want documents *now* on some particular subject of interest. The publisher will just put the magazine or journal or book in the repository, and it will be available. The movement will be one of those ground swells that ignores professional committees and the titanic meetings of Congress and simply happens.

This new system of mine is called Xanadu, which we claim as a trademark, after that magic place of literary memory in Coleridge's great poem "Kubla Khan."

The Future of the Librarian

But now you, the librarians, say, "Wait, what about us, where are we in this transaction?" I don't know! What I am trying to create is a system for rapid access, first to the elite and later to everybody, because I am a *popu*-elitist when it comes to access to the world's heritage and writings.

A vital concern in this electronic system is the issue of preservation. I am desperately concerned for preservation. How do we get these things into authenticated electronic form before they crumble? We will need enabling laws and methods that wiggle around the copyright situation so that if we can't find the copyright holder, somebody has permission to put it in.

So, again, what about libraries? I don't know, because the library has been a common locus of many things, including the storage and preservation for the convenience of a noble prince or noble corporation, a municipality or a nation. A library is a place we put all that "stuff" we are acquiring so we can get to it. Now, when the new place we put it becomes a system of disks and tapes, this changes the nature. Who is in charge of the disks and tapes? Whoever runs the particular facility. If you ask who is in charge of the whole network, then the answer is that no one is in charge. It is a software system that maintains a universal addressed space wherein any document may be located and that may grow indefinitely. Anyone may publish a document by paying one of the service providers.

Who catalogs and categorizes the document? The answer is *"That's your problem!"* So you see, there is something for librarians to do because, as I have said, a catalog and classification represent a point of view. This may seem self-referential because if the catalog is *about* documents, how can it be a document itself? To answer that question, look, for example, at the original designs of the principal cataloging systems. I believe the Library of Congress classification system had a whole major decimal place for "monism" when it was set up. I always wanted to write a book that would be filed under "monism" just to fill that great missing tooth and the lower decimal place because monism isn't considered a subject anymore.

I bought a twenty-year-old computer dictionary recently for two dollars on a table outside a used-book store. Flipping through it I found hardly one concept in it that anyone talks about anymore. Categories and ideas decay. They change because they are points of view. Maintaining the new point of view, staying at the leading edge of everything and rediscovering the fine old ideas that we thought were obsolete in this continual turnover, is the business of literature. Librarians are in the business of categorization, keeping track of the continual turnover of ideas, and of the documents that represent those ideas.

I want to leave you with a sense that all is not lost. You don't have to fight what is coming, nor do you have to believe everything they tell you. The world is still going to be safe for ideas. The world is still going to be a turmoil of new concepts, encapsulated in documents, with pictures and words and three-dimensional walk-through rooms that you will bring to your screen through virtual reality and thousand-track music and sound effects in software. Yet all of these will fall into your lap as the new literature, of which librarians will continue to be the guardians.

Intellectual Preservation
in the
Electronic Environment

Peter S. Graham

Preservation issues are important, as they lie at the heart of the library's mission to provide the human record, the mission that makes librarianship important to me and, I suspect, to many readers of this chapter.[1] The collection of the human record for succeeding generations is the central element of librarianship, the element that distinguishes us from bookstores and entertainment centers. The mission of preservation is central to the professional activities of librarians in collection development, technical services, and special collections. That is why it was an honor to have been invited to be part of the program on this topic that was organized by Arnold Hirshon as president of the Association for Library Collections & Technical Services.

That is also why that audience and this readership have a special responsibility to cope with electronic-preservation issues. The requirements of these technologies will change the way many librarians work in technical services as well as elsewhere in research libraries. And librarians—especially special collections and technical services librarians—are uniquely qualified to take up the technological challenge. If we do not, we will contribute to the stagnation of our own profession as well as fail in our responsibility to history.

Editor's Note: Owing to the illness of one of the originally scheduled speakers, Peter Graham agreed to speak on short notice at the ALCTS President's Program. The substance of his speech was in great measure the same as a paper he delivered at the Preconference of the Rare Books and Manuscripts Section of the Association of College and Research Libraries in Santa Cruz, California, on June 26, 1992. Because this work was so vital to the ALCTS President's Program, Graham graciously agreed to simultaneous publication both in the present *Proceedings* and those of the Rare Books and Manuscripts Preconference.

Preservation until now has been a matter of preserving the artifact that has the work inherent in it, thereby preserving the work itself. Electronic documents, by contrast, force our preservation considerations to divide into two: not only the preservation of the objects as before, but also the preservation of the information contained in those objects, which is now so easily separable from them.

Barry Neavill, a professor at the library school at the University of Alabama, wrote presciently on these topics almost ten years ago that no one had "addressed the issue of the long-term survival of information. . . . The survival of information in an electronic environment becomes an intellectual and technological problem in its own right."[2] He said if we want to assure permanence of the intellectual record that is published electronically, then it will be necessary consciously to design and build the required mechanisms within electronic systems. We still need those mechanisms.

This paper addresses this need in three parts. First, it briefly describes some of the issues associated with preservation of the objects containing electronic information, or the medium preservation. Second, it discusses the challenge of intellectual preservation: the protection and authentication of information that exists in electronic form. Finally, it makes the point that the successful resolution of these issues will require librarianship to change itself or fail to survive as a vital profession.

Medium Preservation

Electronic Information

Electronic information is now a familiar, even integral, part of librarianship. Technical services librarians are among those who are most familiar with it, and many can see what is coming.

Electronic information is commonly available in the marketplace and on the national electronic networks (though the printed book is nowhere near being superseded by electronic texts). Online information services such as Dialog and CD-ROM publications such as *PsycLit* and *InfoTrac* have been around long enough to be called traditional. The *Oxford English Dictionary* is now available in some forms only electronically. There are about a dozen electronic journals with formal peer-review processes, and at least several hundred informal electronic journals and newsletters of interest within the scholarly community.

The *Thesaurus Linguae Graecae* now provides complete electronic texts of the entire corpus of ancient Greek. Charles Chadwyck-Healey has made available for purchase the whole of Migne's *Patrologia Latina;* if we're really lucky we'll get the Greek as well. The Center for Electronic Texts in the Humanities, located at Rutgers and Princeton, is helping scholars gain access to texts of the Library of America, the Oxford Text Archives, the archives maintained by Professor Antonio Zampolli in Pisa, and the Women's Writers Project.

Electronic books are now common. The Bible appeared on floppy disk in the early 1980s. In 1988 Professor Harvey Wheeler of the University of Southern California published what he called an electronic textbook on a floppy disk; it was little more than the ASCII text of his book of about eight chapters. In 1991 the Voyager Company took an interesting step forward by initiating their Extended Book series, with works such as *Alice in Wonderland* and *Pride and Prejudice*, in HyperCard format, including word-searching, note-taking, and place-marking capabilities; the titles are reportedly selling well. The new Modern Library series also will be available on disks.

The next step is interactive electronic books. *Victory Garden* has just been published electronically for $34.95; it is an interactive novel that focuses on the Desert Storm war in Iraq.[3] Robert Coover recently wrote an extensive discussion of hypertext books created with programs such as Guide, HyperCard, and StorySpace; some of the novels arise out of the writing course he teaches at Brown.[4] He provides a bibliography going back to 1987, when what he calls the "landmark" text by Michael Joyce was published, entitled *Afternoon*.[5]

These tips of the electronic iceberg are reminders of the increased frequency with which we come into contact with electronic materials. There may be technical services professionals who will never have to deal with an electronic text; but there are many others who should expect to be managing electronic collections of some kind by the end of the decade. Our concern in preserving materials in such a collection will be similar to today's concern with preserving books: We want to preserve undisturbed as much information as possible for future scholars.

The Book

In the case of books (and I use "books" as a shorthand reference for all printed material and in many cases for manuscript material as well) it is desirable to preserve both the texts contained and the artifactual containers.[6] For some purposes they are inseparable. For example, the most authoritative bibliographic or textual criticism of seminal works requires working with the original publications or manuscripts, for reproductions and facsimiles inevitably introduce some small amount of error. And the resolution of textual problems is sometimes made possible only by examining the physical structures of the actual book, as has long been demonstrated by the study of Shakespeare's texts. It has become a truism that to perceive the earliest or most authoritative manifestation of the work, we must examine and handle artifacts.

For some purposes of textual study we are able to separate study of the work, or text, from study of the artifact. It is practical to do some bibliographic and textual work, at least initially, with a fine facsimile or a good microfilm. In fact, many libraries now provide such surrogates to scholars to obviate unnecessary handling of unique originals. Scholarly editions of classics, to say nothing of popular reprints, make works more widely available than would otherwise be possible if only the original exemplars existed; the work is separated from the artifact for this purpose.

The book itself is sometimes an object of study independently of the text. The study of bindings is a mature field. Some readers will be familiar with the confluence of two other schools of study: British and American bibliography, exemplified by the work of W. W. Greg and Fredson Bowers, and the French school of *l'histoire du livre*, furthered by Lucien Febvre, Henri-Jean Martin, and now Roger Chartier. The text is never very distant, but the focus in these modes of study may be on the artifact or on modes of readership rather than solely on the text.

The Electronic Medium

In the electronic environment it is unlikely that the focus of study will be upon the electronic medium itself. To begin with, there is nothing in an electronic text that necessarily indicates how it was created, and the ease with which electronic texts can be transferred from disk to disk, or networked from computer to computer, means that there is no necessary indication of the source medium or even if the information has been copied at all. We are not likely to see sale catalog references in the future, therefore, that remark on the fine quality of the floppy disk's exterior label or on the electronic text's provenance ("*Moby Dick* on the original Seagate drive; never reformatted, very fine").[7]

The preservation of the information will still require the preservation of whatever medium it is contained on at any given time. This is mostly what has been meant when our profession has discussed electronic preservation. But it has not been enough noticed that there are two kinds of preservation required for information media: one is the preservation of the physical medium on which the information resides, and another is the preservation of the storage technology that makes use of that medium.[8]

The physical preservation of media does not need to be addressed extensively here, for at any given time the physical characteristics of the medium in use are well understood, and the problems inherent in preserving it are simply financial and managerial: who should pay for the necessary equipment and for the properly designed and acclimatized space, how often should backups be made, and who keeps track of backups and sees that they happen.[9] These issues cause expenses for the electronic collection, but they raise only routine technological questions. We can look forward to the proceedings of the Wisconsin Preservation Program held on June 3 and 4, 1992, which will include discussions of data refreshing techniques and of longevity and preservation of magnetic tapes and CD-ROMs.[10]

The storage obsolescence problem is quite another matter. A brief sequence of storage media many of us have seen in our lifetimes would include the following items (an asterisk [*] indicates media that are considered by some to have long-term storage potential):

- punched cards,* in at least three formats (eighty column, ninety column, ninety-six column)
- seven-track half-inch tape* (at densities of 200, 556, and 800 bits per inch)
- nine-track half-inch tape* for mainframes, with various recording modes and densities up to 3200 bpi and beyond
- nine-track half-inch tape cassettes* for mainframes ("square tapes," as they are known in contradistinction to the earlier "round tapes")
- RAMAC disk storage
- magnetic drum storage
- data cell drives*
- removable disk packs*
- Winchester (sealed removable) disk packs*;
- mass storage devices (honeycombs of high-density tape spindles)
- sealed disk drives
- floppy disks* of three sizes so far and at least three storage densities so far
- cartridge tapes* of very high density (e.g., Exabyte) for use in workstation backups and data storage
- removable disk-storage media on PCs
- laser-encoded disks* (CD-ROMs and laser disks)
- magneto-optical disks,* both WORM (write-once-read-many) and rewritable

Some of the storage options appearing now and in the next year include new floppy disk sizes and storage densities and flash cards, or memory cards, for use with very small computers. Under discussion are storage crystals, encoded by laser beams and having the advantage of great capacity without moving parts.

Technologies are superseding each other at a rapid rate. There are already anecdotes of data lost because they can no longer be read by the machines that wrote them: the census data on early tapes, for example, that can only be read by a machine now in the Smithsonian that no longer is functioning. We can be sure that authors and agencies are storing long-term information on floppy disks of all sizes; but we don't know for how long we are going to be able to read them. No competent authorities in librarianship yet express confidence in the long-term storage capabilities or technological life of any present electronic-storage media. An example is CD-ROMs. Their economical use in librarianship derives from their mass-market use for entertainment; that mass market may be threatened by DVI (digital video interactive) technology or others now being actively promoted by entertainment vendors. If forms alternative to CDs win out in entertainment, the production of equipment for CDs and therefore CD-ROMs will be quickly curtailed.

There are perhaps three possible long-term solutions for preserving storage media in the face of obsolescence (as opposed to physical decay), and they vary in practicality: preserve the storage technology, migrate the information to newer technologies, or migrate the information to paper or other long-term eye-readable hard copy.

The prospect for the first option, preserving older technologies, is not bright: Equipment ages and breaks, documentation disappears, vendor support vanishes, and the storage medium as well as the equipment deteriorates.

For the second option, migration, there is a lifeline of hope provided by a consistency that has so far remained through all these medium changes: the 8-bit byte and its multiples. Since the byte's serious introduction by IBM's System/360 series in April 1964, other memory-unit sizes have fallen into desuetude. There is now agreement, for the very basic characters of the English alphabet and numbers and some common signs, on the first 128 characters that can be described by the 8 bits. This agreement is codified as the character set we know as ASCII (American Standard Code for Information Interchange). There are extensions creating a 2-byte character set for global-language handling—for example, for the Asian ideographic scripts such as Japanese and Chinese that Apple has recently announced—but the first 128 bit combinations remain the ASCII standard.

What this means is that most character-based data could be preserved by migrating them from one storage medium to another as the medium becomes decrepit or obsolete. Doing this requires a computer that can read in the old mode and write in the new; with present network capabilities this is usually not difficult to arrange.

Whether transfer from one medium to another is practical for large quantities of information over long periods of time is another matter. The investment necessary to migrate files of data will involve skilled labor, complex record keeping, physical piece management, checks for successful outcomes, space, and equipment. The effort required for an orderly photocopying of books in the collection every ten years is at the right order of magnitude of data-migration costs and complexities. And in any case, this migration solution would only work for ASCII text data. Migrating graphic, image, moving, or sound data, or even formatted text, will only work as long as the software application can also be migrated to the next computing platform.

The third option—practical but unexciting—is to migrate information from high-technology electronic form to stable hard copy, either paper or microform. In the near term, for certain classes of high-value archival material, this is likely to be the permanent medium of choice. It offers known long life, eye readability, and freedom from technological obsolescence. It also, of course, discards the flexibility in use and transport of information in electronic form.

Migration to hard copy is of no use for one new class of electronic information, the interactive document. Those familiar with hypertext applications—for example, HyperCard on the Macintosh—will understand that simply to print out the information contained in a hypertext file is to lose much of the point of having created the file in the first place. An example is *Victory Garden*, or the NewBook Company's instructional document in ethics *Warsaw 1939*.[11] Using this program the reader chooses which character to be and at various points must choose options available to that character—for example, fleeing Warsaw or staying with one's family, turning over hostages to the SS or refusing to do so. The cumulative effect of these decisions determines outcomes that would be impossible to show on the printed page.

Intellectual Preservation

The Problem

The more challenging problem is intellectual preservation—preserving not just the medium on which information is stored, but the information itself. Electronic information must be dealt with separately from its medium, much more so than with books, because electronic information is so easily transferable. Patricia Wilson Berger deserves credit for calling attention, in her inaugural speech as ALA president in 1989, to the security and integrity of electronic data as one of the foundations of information access:

> In a democracy, information access requires an information base secure from intrusion, distortion, and destruction; one protected from both physical and technological deterioration.[12]

The presidential committee on preservation that she appointed reported its results in 1991. Unfortunately, while it noted in passing the need for document integrity, it focused on the medium when speaking of electronic preservation. (It did note and affirm the centrality of preservation to librarianship.)[13]

The need to focus on the two issues separately arises because the great asset of digital information is also its great liability: The ease with which an identical copy can be quickly and flawlessly made is paralleled by the ease with which a copy may be made with an undetectable flaw. Neavill wrote prophetically in 1984 of the "malleability" of electronic information, that is, its ability to be easily transformed and manipulated.[14]

The problem may be put in the form of several questions that confront the user of any electronic document (whether it is text, graphic, numeric, or multimedia information) because the problems are similar. How can I be sure that what I am reading is what I want to read? How do I know that the document I have found is the same one that you read and made reference to in your bibliography? How can I be sure that the document I am reading has not been changed since it was created or since the last time I read it? To put it most generally: How can a reader be sure that the document being used is the one intended?

We properly take for granted the fixity of text in the print world: The printed journal article I examine because of the footnote you gave is beyond question the same text that you read. Therefore we have confidence that our discussion is based upon a common foundation. The present state of electronic texts is such that we no longer can have that confidence.

Taxonomy of Changes

There are three possibilities of change or damage that electronic texts can undergo that confront us with the need for intellectual preservation (note again that only modification is specifically addressed; complete loss or deletion presents different problems):

- accidental change
- intended change (well meant)
- intended change that is not well meant, that is, fraud

Accidental Change.   A document can sometimes be damaged accidentally, perhaps by data loss during transfer or through inadvertent mistakes in manipulation. For example, data may be corrupted in being sent over a network or between disks and memory on a computer; this happens seldom, but it is possible.[15]

More likely is the loss of sections of a document or a whole version of a document resulting from accidents in updating. For example, if a document exists in multiple versions, or drafts, the latest version (N) might be lost, leaving only a previous version (N - 1). Many of us have had this experience. It is easy for the casual reader, or even the author, not to notice that text has been lost in this way.

Just as common in word processing is the experience of incorrectly updating the original version that was supposed to be retained in pristine form. In such a case only the earlier version (N - 1), if it still exists, and the incorrectly updated version (N + 1) remain; again, a reader or author may not be aware of the difference. Note that in both cases backup mechanisms and the need for them are not the issue, but rather how we know which version we have or don't have.

Intended Change (Well Meaning).   There are at least three possibilities for well-meaning change. The changes might result in a specific new version, they might be a structural update that is normal and expected, or they might be the normal outcome of an interactive document.

New versions and drafts are familiar to us from dealing with authorial texts, for example, or from working with legislative bills or with revisions of working papers. It is desirable to keep track bibliographically of the distinction between one version and another. We are accustomed to drafts being numbered and edition statements being explicit, and original catalogers expend significant effort on descriptions to make distinctions clear.

We are accustomed to visual cues to tell us when a version is different; in addition to explicit numbering we observe the page format, the typos, the producer's name, the binding, the paper itself. These cues are not dependable for distinguishing electronic versions, for many of them can vary for identical informational texts when produced in hard copies. It is for this reason that the Text Encoding Initiative Guidelines Project has called for indications of version change in electronic texts even when a single character has been changed.[16]

It is important to know the difference between versions so that our discussion is properly founded; I disagree with Harvey Wheeler, a professor at the University of Southern California, who is enthusiastic about what he calls a "dynamic document" that continually reflects the development of an author's thinking.[17] Scholars and readers need to know what the changes are and when they are made.

Structural updates, changes that are inherent in the document, also cause changes in information content. A dynamic database by its nature is frequently updated, such as *Books in Print*, for example, or a university personnel directory (*White Pages*). Boilerplate such as a funding proposal might also be updated often by various authors. In each of these cases it is appropriate and expected for the information to change constantly.[18] Yet it is also appropriate for the information to be shared and analyzed at a given point in time. In print form, for example, *Books in Print* gives us a historical record of printing in the United States; the directory tells us who was a member of the university in a given year. In electronic form there is no historical record unless a snapshot is taken at a given point in time. How do we identify that snapshot and authenticate it at a later time?[19]

Another form of well-meaning change occurs in interactive documents. I have already mentioned the interactive capabilities of *Warsaw 1939*, the note-taking capabilities of the Voyager Extended Books, and the interactive HyperCard novels described by Coover. We can expect someone to want snapshots of these documents, inadequate though they may be. We need an authoritative way to distinguish one snapshot from another.

Intended Change (Fraud).   The third kind of change that can occur is intentional change for fraudulent reasons. The change might be of one's own work, to cover one's tracks or change evidence for a variety of reasons, or it might be damage to the work of another. In an electronic future the opportunities for a Stalinist revision of history will be multiplied. An unscrupulous researcher could change experimental data without a trace. A financial dealer might wish to cover tracks to hide improper business, or a political figure might wish to hide or modify inconvenient earlier views.

Imagine that the only evidence of the Iran-Contra scandal or the only record of Bill Clinton's draft-board correspondence was in electronic mail. Consider the political benefit that might derive if each of the parties could modify their own past correspondence without detection. Then consider the case if each of them could modify the other's correspondence without detection. We need a defense against both cases.

Solutions

The solution is to fix a text or document in some way so that a user can be sure of the original text when it is needed. This solution is called authentication, which is very important in the business, political, and espionage communities. Once again libraries can take advantage of technology developed for other purposes. There are three important electronic techniques used for authentication: cryptography, hashing, and time-stamping.

Encryption.   The two best-known forms of cryptography are DES and RSA. The DES (Data Encryption Standard) was first established about 1975 and adopted by many business and government agencies. The RSA is an encryption process developed by three mathematicians from MIT (*R*ivest, *S*hamir, and *A*dleman) at about the same time and marketed privately; it is regarded by many as superior to the DES.[20]

Encryption depends upon mathematical transformation of a document. The transformation uses a standard process, a computation algorithm, that establishes a particular number as the basis of the computation. This number, or key, is also required to decode the resulting encrypted text; the key is typically many digits long, perhaps one hundred or more. Modern encryption depends upon the process being so complex that decoding by chance or merely human effort is impossible. It also depends upon the difficulty of decoding by brute-force computational trial-and-error methods; these would take unreasonably long periods of time, perhaps hundreds or thousands of years, even using modern supercomputers.

Therefore, the key, which is crucial to encryption, is also the problem because passing the key to authorized persons turns out to be the Achilles' heel of the process. How is the key sent to someone: on paper in the mail or by messenger? These introduce the usual vulnerabilities dramatized in thriller literature. Do you send the key electronically? Sending it as plain text doesn't seem like a good idea, and sending it in encrypted form—well, you see the problem. This is a recognized flaw in the widely used DES encryption method.

The RSA encryption technique is called public-key cryptography: It uses a public key and a private key. The computational algorithm used for encrypting depends upon a specific pair of numbers; data encoded by one number cannot be decoded using the same number but can only be decoded by the other number; and vice versa.

In figure 1, a user, let's say Rita, keeps one of the pair of numbers secret as a private key and makes the other number available as a public key. The public key can be used by anyone, (such as her friend Art) to send coded messages to Rita. Only Rita can decode the message because only she has the other number of the pair. She sends an encrypted message back to Art using not her private key, but Art's public key, and only he can decode it, mutatis mutandis.

Alternatively, Rita can code a simple message using her private key, and anyone else can decode it using her public key. This functions as a digital signature, allowing her messages to be authenticated, since only she is able to create such messages. The usefulness is evident in financial transfers, for example, or in authenticating electronic mail or electronic purchase orders.

Encryption in either form, however, is not likely to be an authentication system desirable for library use. Encryption offers the possibility of authenticating a text, but only if the text has not been changed and reencrypted. Encryption also has several drawbacks. No matter which method is used, encryption requires keys specific to the reader and writer. If the keys are generally available, which is necessary for wide document access, then authentication is not possible, because the document could easily be modified and reencrypted using the same keys. In addition, one of our library concerns is authentication over periods of time that are even longer than a normal human lifetime. Secret keys may be lost over such periods of time, making encrypted documents useless.

Hashing.   Another technique is called hashing; it is a shorthand means by which we can establish the uniqueness of a document. Hashing depends upon the assignment of arbitrary values to each portion of the document and thence upon the resulting computation of specific but

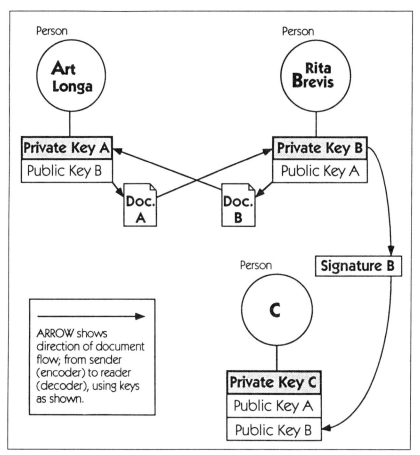

FIGURE 1.   Public Key Encryption

contentless values called hash totals or hashes. It is "contentless" because the specific computed hash total has no value other than itself; in particular, it is impossible or infeasible to compute backward from the hash to the original document. The hash may be a number of a hundred digits or so, but it is much shorter than the document from which it was computed. Thus a hash has several virtues: It is much smaller than the original document, it preserves the privacy of the original document, and it uniquely describes the original document.

Figure 2 provides a simplified description of how a hash is created. If each letter is assigned a value from 1 to 26, then a word will have a numeric total if its letters are summed. In the first example, "eat" has a value of 26. The problem is, the word "tea" (composed of the same letters) has the same value in this scheme. The scheme can be made more complicated, as shown in the second pair of examples, if the letter values are also multiplied by a

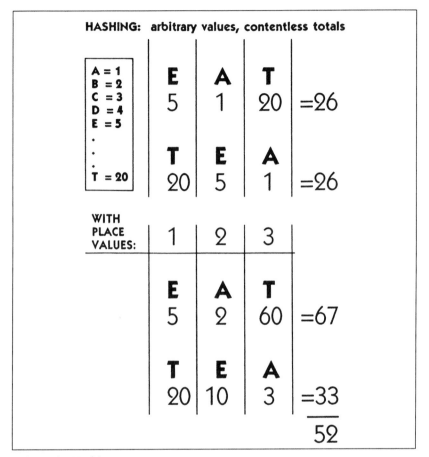

FIGURE 2. Hashing

place value. In this scheme, the two words of the same letters end up with different totals. For the sake of illustration, the numbers at the right are shown as summed to the value 52 at the bottom; in fact the total is 152, but the leftmost digit can be discarded without materially affecting the fact that a specific hash total has been found: contentless, private, and (in this simple example) reasonably distinctive of the particular words in the "document."

This is a very simplistic description of a process that can be made excessively complicated for human computation. It remains easy for current computing technology to compute quite complex hashes for any kind of document; paradoxically, these hashes are beyond the reach of supercomputers to falsify or break for the perceived future. Hashing as a means of authentication is a topic of interest to the business and government communities, and there have been several recent mathematical papers on it, including descriptions of recent patents.

How might libraries use hashing as an authentication technique? First, we would have to adopt a standard hashing algorithm (a computational method) that we trust. Second, the algorithm must be widely distributable in a useful form, probably as a menu or hot-key command on a microcomputer. The selected algorithm is likely to be commercially licensed. Fortunately, those talking about creating such an authentication tool want it to be so cheap that it is easy to hash documents at will; thus the likelihood is for the algorithm of choice to be inexpensive or even free. It is typical for a document to be mundane at the time of its creation; it is only later that a document becomes important. Therefore, an authentication mechanism is needed that is so cheap and easy that documents can be authenticated as a matter of routine.

In this scheme, each time a document or a draft is created or saved, the hash is created, saved with it, and is separately retrievable. If the document is electronically published, it should be published with its hash; and if the document is cited, the hash should be part of the citation. If a reader using the document wishes to know if she has the right one, she computes the hash easily on her own computer using the standard algorithm and compares it with the published hash. If they are the same, she has confidence that she has the correct, untampered version of the document before her.

Time-Stamping.   Electronic time-stamping takes the process a step further. Time-stamping is a means of authenticating not only a document, but its existence at a specific time. It is analogous to rubber-stamping incoming mail with the date and time it was received. An electronic technique has been developed by Stuart Haber and Scott Stornetta, two researchers at Bellcore in New Jersey.[21] Their efforts initially were prompted by charges of intellectual fraud made against a biologist, and they became interested in how to demonstrate that there had been no tampering with the electronic evidence. In addition, they were aware that their technique could be useful as a means for determining priority of thought (for example, in the patenting process) so that electronic claims for intellectual priority could be unambiguously made.

The Haber and Stornetta technique depends on a mathematical procedure involving the entire specific contents of the document, which means they have provided a tool for determining change as well as for fixing the date of the document. A great advantage of their procedure is that it is entirely public, except (if desired) for the contents of the document itself. Thus it is very useful for the library community, which wishes to keep documents available rather than hide them, and which needs to do so over periods of time beyond those it can immediately control.

The time-stamping process envisioned by Haber and Stornetta depends upon hashing as the first step. Assume, in figure 3, that author A

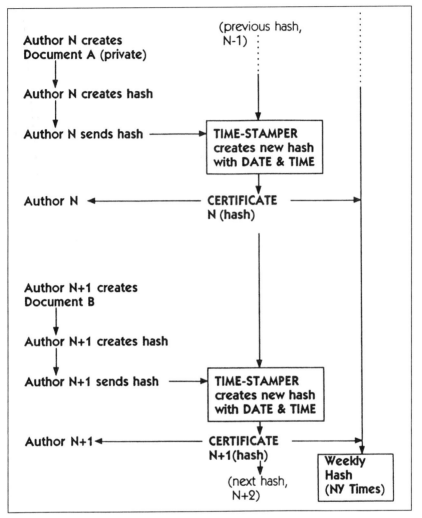

FIGURE 3.   Time-Stamping

creates document A and wishes to establish it as of a certain time. First he creates a hash for document A using a standard, publicly available program. He then sends this hash over the network to a time-stamping server. Note that he has thus preserved the privacy of his document for as long as he wishes, as it is only the hash that is sent to the server. The time-stamping server uses standard, publicly available software to combine this hash with two other numbers: a hash from the just previous document that it has authenticated, and a hash derived from the current time and date. The resulting number is called a certificate, and the server returns this certificate to author A. The author now preserves this certificate, a number, and

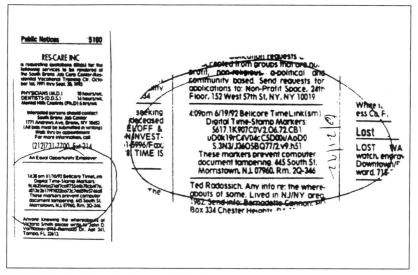

FIGURE 4.   Public and Commercial Notices

transmits it with document A and uses it when referring to document A (e.g., in a bibliography) to distinguish it from other versions of the document.

The time-stamping server has one other important function: It combines the certificate hash with others for that week into a number that, once a week, is published in the personals column of the *New York Times* ("Commercial and Public Notices"), as in figure 4. The public nature of this number assures that there can be no tampering with it.

The privacy of the document has been preserved for as long as author A wishes; there is also no other secrecy in this process. All steps are taken in public using available programs and procedures. Note, too, that no other document will result in the same certificate, for document A's certificate is dependent not only upon the algorithms and upon the document's hash total, but upon the hash of the particular and unpredictable document that was immediately previous. Once document A has been authenticated, it becomes itself the previous document for the authentication of document B.

Now let us consider reader C, who wishes to determine the authenticity of the electronic document before her. Perhaps it is an electronic press release from a senatorial campaign or an electronic funds transfer, or perhaps it is the year 2092 and the document is an electronic text of author A. Reader C has available the certificate for document A. If she can validate that number from the document she can be sure she has the authenticated contents. Using the standard software, she re-creates the hash for the document and sends the hash over the network, with the certificate, to the time-stamping server. The server reports back on the validity of the certificate for that document.

But let us suppose that it is the year 2092 and the server is nowhere to be found. Reader C then searches out the microfilm of the *New York Times* for the putative date of the document in question and determines the published hash number. Using that number and the standard software, she tests the authenticity of her document just as the server would.

What I have described are simplified forms of methods for identifying a unique document and for authenticating a document as created at a specific point in time with a specific content. Whether the specific tools of hashing or time-stamping are those the library community will use in the future is open to question. It is, however, the first time librarians have been offered electronic authentication tools that provide generality, flexibility, ease of use, openness, low cost, and functionality over long periods of time on the human scale. When using such tools (or similar ones yet to be developed), a user can have confidence that the document being read is the one desired or intended and that it has not been altered without the reader's being aware of it.

Role of Librarians

Why do this? Why bother? The answer to these questions should be self-evident: It is what we librarians do. The basic paradigm of librarianship taught in library school is to acquire information, organize it, preserve it, and make it available. This has been a useful and instructive paradigm in dealing with print materials, and it continues to be useful and instructive as we consider electronic information.

The preservation imperative should be particularly important for readers of this article. In research libraries, and not only in special collections, the consideration of long periods of time is more important than in other library fields. It is our particular responsibility to see that we preserve and organize materials for use not only by our generation but by succeeding generations of scholars and students. No one else has this specific responsibility; it is what we do. If we do not do it, no one else will.

Pessimistically speaking, it is possible that the job cannot be done. We may be swimming against the tide. Sociologically, our society is obsessed with the present and uncaring of the past and therefore of its records. Technologically refined tools are now available that not only allow but encourage the quick and easy modification of text, of pictures, and of sounds. It is becoming routine to produce ad hoc versions of performances and to produce technical reports in tailored versions on demand. The technology that allows us to interact with information is itself inhibiting us from preserving our interaction.

However, there is cause for optimism. In our house there are many mansions; there will continue to be people who want history, who care about the human record, and who will support our efforts to serve them. Some aspects of electronic preservation are already being dealt with by other communities. The financial and business communities, for example, have a stake in authentication of electronic communication. The business and computing communities in general are interested in protecting against the undesired loss of data in the short term. The government and business communities have an interest in the security of systems.

But there is no other professional group dealing with the combination of all these issues—authentication, security, and protection—as complicated by the length of time in centuries, which research librarians contemplate, and by the need to provide organized access to what is preserved.

Some librarians may draw back from the apparent complexity of the technologies that support electronic information. But these technologies should present no difficulty to minds that can easily deal with corporate authorship and with the acquisition of monographic continuations. The capacity for creating and using the MARC record is adequate to the task of setting up standards for electronic preservation. Providing valid electronic authentication techniques is no more intractable than the problem of providing holdings statements for works in multiple formats.

The traditional form of technical services is becoming stale and is in danger of becoming a personnel backwater as what it does becomes more and more routine. There is difficulty already in finding technical services staff, especially catalogers, who have the skills, judgment, and management ability needed. I have written elsewhere that one of the ways the function of technical services within librarianship will reinvigorate itself is by taking on the technological challenges.[22] The skills formerly devoted to the cataloging code and to authority control are ideally suited to working with very technologically complex material.

Technical services librarians, like special collections librarians, are used to dealing professionally with the "knotty problems," the ones invisible to patrons but requiring solutions to support their needs: the tough issues that require analysis, intellectual clarity, marshaling of allies, and persuasive, energetic leadership. Understanding and implementing electronic access and preservation will lead to increased sophistication within our staffs on systems, hardware and software, technologies, networking, and data transfer. It will also lead to increased sophistication about legal issues, technology transfer, intellectual property, and information provision. These knotty problems will actually aid us in attracting the staff we need and keeping the ones we have: They will want to rise to the new challenges.

Many librarians in technical services are working with the new technologies already. The terminology of DOS, 80486 chips, PageMaker, file transfer protocols (FTP), and thin-wire Ethernet is part of library language. Those of us (most of us) working with electronic mail, newsgroups, listservs, and Gophers are very aware of the technology and increasingly aware of how we need to manage it.

And it is managing that is necessary. There are technical people aplenty who can grapple with the bits and bytes of these issues if librarians give them proper direction. The need is for someone to articulate the requirements for the electronic preservation of the human record and to lead our profession in making it happen. That is the professional requirement, and it is the people reading this—you—who are the most capable of assuring that it does happen. There is a kind of back-to-basics quality to our confronting the electronic environment: To grapple with the ephemerality of electronic information is to answer the abstract question of why we are librarians.

Most of us know that we like books; readers of this article are likely to appreciate books as physical objects and to enjoy reading. Technical services and collection development librarians often handle particularly attractive books and important texts (sometimes they are even the same). But back to basics. Our social value as librarians comes from our provision of information—our locating it, organizing it, and preserving it. Libraries, and technical services, will change. The change will be affected by how well we stick to our past, that is, by how we propose to carry on professional activities. If we continue to emphasize only the physical objects we know as books, important as they are, then a museum role becomes increasingly likely as we become marginal to the real scholarly communication now going on.

Alternatively, we can continue to emphasize our professional obligation to preserve and make available the human record, regardless of its form. Then we can lay claim to being a part of the very current affairs of our society, our universities, and to the resources we need to carry out this obligation. Finding ways to do all of this is our professional requirement.

Notes

1. Patricia Wilson Berger, 1989–90 ALA president, emphasized just this point in the electronic context in her inaugural speech as noted below.

Patricia Glass Schuman, 1991–92 ALA president, based her year of activities on the "right to know"; the preservation of knowledge, regardless of form, is an integral part of the citizenry's right to knowledge.

(I want gratefully to acknowledge the continuing encouragement to prepare this paper of Robert S. Martin of the Louisiana State University Libraries, program chair of the 1992 RBMS preconference, at which this paper was first given.)

2. Gordon B. Neavill, "Electronic Publishing, Libraries, and the Survival of Information," *Library Resources & Technical Services* 28 (Jan. 1984): 78.

3. Stuart Moulthrop, *Victory Garden* (Cambridge, Mass.: Eastgate Systems, 1991). This is an 800MB disc for the Macintosh, signed and numbered 226/250 by author, plus a sixteen-page brochure with an introduction by Michael Joyce and explanatory matter, all in plastic casing labeled "first edition."

4. Robert Coover, "The End of Books," *New York Times Book Review*, June 21, 1992, 1, 23–25.

5. Michael Joyce, *Afternoon: A Story* (Cambridge, Mass.: Eastgate Systems, 1987). I have not yet seen this item.

6. The Commission on Preservation and Access takes the lead in asserting the very reasonable view that in many cases to preserve the work we must sacrifice the artifact (e.g., in guillotining for microfilming). The absolute view in opposition, which must also be heard, is cogently stated by G. Thomas Tanselle in his sixth Sol M. Malkin lecture, *Libraries, Museums, and Reading* (New York: Book Arts Press, 1991).

7. But how can we be sure what future uses scholars will make of this infant technology? And see in note 3 the description of *Victory Garden*, which I saw only after this talk was originally given.

8. There is a third kind, the obsolescence of software designed to read a specific medium. For example, Kathleen Kluegel has pointed out how CD-ROM (Compact Disc—Read-Only Memory) software updates have left unreadable older discs of the same published database. She fears CD-ROM's ending up "being the 8-track tape of the information industry" in "CD-ROM Longevity," message on PACS-L (listserv@uhupvm1.bitnet, April 29, 1992).

9. For example, there have been flurries of hope for long-term storage using CD-ROMs. Vendors solved early problems that led to quick deterioration of some CD-ROMs: Apparently, for example, if oxygen gets inside the sealed disk the aluminum substrate deteriorates rapidly, and some early disks were not properly sealed. More recently, some vendors were predicting one-hundred-year lives for CD-ROMs (Barry Fox, "CD Makers Perform in Unison to Stop the Rot," *New Scientist* 134 (Apr. 4, 1992): 19). The using community, including libraries, is still undecided whether lives longer than five to ten years can be reasonably expected; and the money-back guarantee of the one-hundred-year vendor does not in itself inspire confidence.

10. "WISPPR Electronic Preservation Conference Report," *ALCTS Network News* 3, no. 29 (June 18, 1992); also summarized in Janice Mohlenrich, "Electronic Preservation Conference," *ALCTS Newsletter* 3, no. 6 (1992): 71–72.

11. Collegium for Research in Interactive Technologies, *Warsaw 1939* (San Diego: Chariot Software Group, 1990). These are two 800MB discs for the Macintosh, plus an eighty-six-page brochure with texts and instructions, with running title "Reader's Guide"; brochure title page lists "Center for Research . . ." as author, though internally and on discs "Collegium" is used.

Production of this instructional work was partially funded by the Annenberg/CPB Project. As a result of its interactive form *Warsaw 1939* is the first computer document that has emotionally stirred me. It deserves to be collected and preserved—but how?

12. As quoted in "Patricia Wilson Berger Inaugurated as ALA President," *Library Hotline* 18, no. 27 (July 10, 1989): 1.

13. "ALA President's Committee on Preservation Policy: Report," *ALCTS Network News* 2, no. 1 (July 8, 1991), a publication "available only in electronic form" by requesting "sub alcts" from listserv@uicvm.bitnet; s.v. subheads "Recommendations . . ." and "Discussion of Preservation Issues."

14. Neavill, 1984, 77.

15. Microcomputers and workstations, unlike mainframe computers, usually do not have sophisticated error detection built in (e.g., parity bits), as the dependability of modern circuitry has not warranted the cost on such commodity items; therefore, when the rare bit is dropped it will not be noticed by the hardware. Some manufacturers do make available parity-checking versions of their microcomputers at 10 percent to 20 percent additional cost.

16. TEI P1, Guidelines, Version 1.1: Chapter 4, "Bibliographic Control, Encoding Declarations and Version Control" (Draft Version 1.1, Oct. 1990); sec. 4.1.6, Revision History, 55: "If the file changes at all, even if only by the correction of a single typographic error, the change should be mentioned. . . . The principle here is that any researcher using the file, including the person who made the changes, should be able to find a record of the history of the file's contents."

17. Harvey Wheeler, keynote speech at the October 1988 LITA conference (Boston). The issue arises in a different context in the note 19.

18. A peculiar case is the transportation timetable. Theoretically it could be dynamically updated in electronic form, yet it is the timetable's hard-copy publication that signals to the users that a change has occurred.

19. An electronic catalog is a similar case. We have never pretended that our card catalogs were static, but the electronic catalogs (particularly when on the network) are so accessible as to raise citation problems. Hugh Amory, a Harvard rare books cataloger, in a review of *Searching the Eighteenth Century* (London: British Library, 1983), responds to Robin Alston's claim of superiority for the Eighteenth Century Short Title Catalog (ESTC) on the grounds that "machine-readable data . . . can be always provisional," by noting: "The permanence of print has its own advantages, moreover: who will wish to cite a catalogue that can change without notice?" (*Papers of the Bibliographical Society of America [PBSA]* 79 (1985): 130).

20. A description of DES is in FIPS Publication 46-1: National Bureau of Standards, *Data Encryption Standard* (Jan. 1988). The RSA Data Security, from whom information is available about their product, is at 10 Twin Dolphin Drive, Redwood City, CA 94065; the original description of RSA's method is in R. L. Rivest, A. Shamir, and L. Adleman, "A Method for Obtaining Digital Signatures and Public-key Cryptosystems," *Communications of the ACM* 21, no. 2 (Feb. 1978): 120–26.

A few readily available popular articles on the two schemes include John Markoff, "A Public Battle over Secret Codes," *New York Times,* May 7, 1992, D1; Michael Alexander, "Encryption Pact in Works," *Computerworld* 25, no. 15 (Apr. 15, 1991); G. Pascal Zachary, "U.S. Agency Stands in Way of Computer-Security Tool," *Wall Street Journal,* July 9, 1990); D. James Bidzos and Burt S. Kaliski, Jr., "An Overview of Cryptography," *LAN Times* (Feb. 1990). More technical and with many references is W. Diffie, "The First Ten Years of Public-key Cryptography," *Proceedings of the IEEE* 76, no. 5 (May 1988): 560–77.

21. Stuart Haber and W. Scott Stornetta, *How to Time-stamp a Digital Document,* DIMACS Technical Report 90-80 (Morristown, N.J.: Dec. 1990). DIMACS is the Center for Discrete Mathematics and Theoretical Computer Science, "a cooperative project of Rutgers University, Princeton University, AT&T Bell Laboratories and Bellcore." The authors are Bellcore employees. Dave Bayer, Stuart Haber, and W. Scott Stornetta, "Improving the Efficiency and Reliability of Digital Time-stamping," *Sequences '91: Methods in Communication, Security, and Computer Science,* ed. R. M. Capocelli (Springer-Verlag, forthcoming).

A brief popular account of this time-stamping method is in John Markoff, "Experimenting with an Unbreachable Electronic Cipher," *New York Times,* Jan. 12, 1992, F9.

22. Peter S. Graham, "Electronic Information and Research Library Technical Services," *College & Research Libraries* 51 (May 1990): 241–50.

Librarians on a Tightrope: Getting from Here to There and Loosening Up in the Process

Susan K. Martin

The topic of choice for librarianship, as well as for other professions these days, seems to be the profession's vision of itself for the future, combined with considerable breast-beating about the current status. In reflecting on this issue for the library profession, it is useful, and often amusing, to consider the ways in which some authors have depicted libraries, or at least the information function, in the distant future. Look at "Star Trek." Have you ever seen a librarian on the *Enterprise?* No—there is a computer to which one can address questions, which are answered, usually, but not to one's satisfaction. The computer is the library *and* the librarian combined; if you want public service and unobtrusive questioning, don't go to the *Enterprise!* As Agnes Griffen said in her article about libraries in science fiction a few years ago, in the robotic library "librarians are noticeable in their absence. The end user is in control."[1]

About ten years ago, when I was working with the staff of the Johns Hopkins library to define its scenario for the future, we described a concept that is a commonplace idea today: the virtual library, or the user deriving information and services from the library without setting foot in the building. Some of the reference librarians were very nervous about this concept; they thought that it would make them obsolete. While I reassured them that this was not the case, I also pointed out that it would be up to them to define their own roles in this new environment and to develop the niche that would cause information seekers to recognize a value added by the reference service.

To achieve this, we need to discuss what public services librarians want and expect from future information-retrieval systems and what the roles and responsibilities of library administrators need to be to help change the

39

current organizational and operational environment. While the focus of this discussion is on those two groups of people, the concerns apply to the entire profession. *In general*, if you ask a public services librarian what he or she wants and expects from future information-retrieval systems, the response will be phrased in terms of more sophisticated searching tools, Boolean logic, more databases, and the ability to incorporate citation databases into the online catalog. That's not very farsighted, and that's an issue to which I will refer later.

If one were to suggest what library administrators *expect* their roles are in changing the organizational and operational environments within which we work, the response would be similar: *In general*, most administrators don't go around thinking in innovative ways about how their organizational and operational environments should change. Rather, they assume either a traditional or a slowly evolving library and often think that changes are going to come from without, rather than from within, the library. "We are being done to" rather than "we are doing."

These two generalizations are exactly that, of course; there are many public services librarians who are way ahead of most of the rest of us, including the library users, in their capacity to imagine new and better information-retrieval systems. Many library administrators spend most if not all of their time trying to change, improve, and reformulate their organizational and operational environments. But a general impression, supported by responses of many librarians and users, is that these farsighted people are in the minority.

Some basic assumptions are used for the purposes of this analysis. These are the following:

- Information will continue to be published in print on paper.
- There will be more electronic informati
- There will be more multimedia publishing.
- There will be more transactional charges for information.
- There will not be more disposable income in the near future.
- We can shape our own destiny, individually and collectively.

The last point requires emphasis. Let's look again at the two major questions under discussion: What do and should public services librarians *want and expect?* What do the *roles and responsibilities* of library administrators need to be to *help change* their environments? The most important task for both public services librarians and administrators is to create their own futures consistent with quality service to information seekers and users: to cause circumstances and conditions to change rather than passively let it happen to libraries or librarians.

We do want to play the information game, after all. Let us look at some of the characteristics that suggest today's conditions: the continuing information explosion; a lingering rotten economy; the development of an information elite, whether we like it or not; the movement of information seekers to find information themselves rather than go to librarians for assistance; and the marvelous technical developments that are represented by Ted Nelson's Project Xanadu and others. As a group, librarians have decided to ally themselves with and to support the information poor within this framework. That is a necessary condition, but it is not a sufficient condition for librarianship to survive and thrive in the future.

To repeat, we want to play the game: We want to be the information guides, the coordinators of publishing, the guardians of access to information. On college campuses, we want to be the managers of the campuswide information systems, but unless we organize to create such systems, someone else on campus will get there first. If we believe that many of the technological developments in information access are someone else's job, that will become a self-fulfilling prophecy. We must recognize that our passivity makes us a slow-moving profession, and that passivity must be overcome. We are so passive that the people we define as our partners often don't even remember that we are here. But we may have a leg up on other professions, most of whom don't even realize that they will require a paradigm shift.

Visions

In mid-1991, something remarkable happened. On the electronic list server called LIBADMIN, a discussion took place about education for librarianship that led to a suggestion at the grassroots level that librarians should develop a strategic vision statement that could be conveyed to other librarians and library school educators, who would then know what kind of people we believe we need for the successful future of the profession. The strategic visions discussion struck a responsive chord, and someone suggested a meeting at ALA last year. The topic resounds; a large number of programs and committees at the ALA meeting in 1992 were concerned with reshaping the profession. Eighty-five people attended that 1991 meeting. The Council on Library Resources, also responding positively, made it possible to create a group we called the Strategic Visions Steering Committee and is stimulating the funding of professionwide activities to improve the positioning of librarianship in the information age.

Just an aside here. For the purposes of strategic visions, the "group" is defined as the entire profession, or at least anyone who wishes to be involved in this effort to reconceptualize librarianship. However, there seemed to be a need for a limited corporate entity, to allow recognition at a level between a single individual and the entire profession. Twenty-eight people, representing all kinds of libraries, are on the steering committee, which has met twice and is intended to stimulate the conversation further but to have a limited life span. It is not affiliated with any professional group.

At its meeting in December 1991, the Strategic Visions Steering Committee continued, in a somewhat more formal manner, to develop a redefinition of the library profession for an age in which information in all forms and formats will be increasingly valuable, and the skills that librarians possess will be required actively by information users. The group agreed that librarians themselves must provide the vision that will allow the potential of the profession to be realized. They drafted a visions statement and an expression of professional values. These documents have been distributed widely and were discussed at many library association meetings during 1992. The ideas presented in the visions statement in particular are relevant to the questions raised earlier about public service librarians and library administrators; it seemed appropriate to bring together these questions with the visions statement to attempt to provide guidance.

Public services librarians and administrators alike will be able to design appropriate information systems for the future and change and mold their organizations by using these principles or some version of them.

The vision establishes the basis for librarianship in the twenty-first century through service, leadership, innovation, and recruitment. All these areas are pertinent to today's concern, and all of them are relevant to both the public services librarians and the administrators. Each part of the visions statement (shown below in italics) can be used to advantage in providing the information services of the future or in administering the information center of the future.[2]

Service Requirements

The service vision goes to the heart of public service issues and suggests that librarians should become more assertive in the way that they approach information and users alike. It proposes a heavy emphasis on the quality of the work that we do: Performance reports that reference questions are answered correctly as little as 50 percent of the time will be unacceptable in the future (if indeed they are at all acceptable today). The concept of user self-sufficiency makes its way into these visions, although not without some struggle. Some of us feel strongly that users must be even more reliant on the librarian than they are now; others feel that the clear direction is toward systems that are easy to use, allowing librarians to concentrate on those questions or users that require more attention or expertise.

Select and deliver information that users need at the point and moment of need. Librarians involved in public services and collection development will be actively engaged not only in developing a collection or providing access to information, but also in understanding in-depth the community served by the library and its potential need for information. Librarians will match that understanding with an up-to-date knowledge of information availability. As an example, Radio Free Europe information has been available online for some time. I met a librarian who was very excited about this daily service and wanted to offer it on a bulletin board on her campus. On investigating the need, she found that the faculty members who most needed that information had known about its availability for months and were already subscribing to the service independent of the library. Had she been in closer contact with both the users and the information, she might have been able to provide the bridge—information at the point and moment of need. We have traditionally thought of ourselves as being the ones who know the most about locating information; this may no longer be true, if it ever was.

Create and maintain systems that provide accurate and reliable information. We talk about being the knowledge providers, the people whose expertise is in the finding and organizing of information. This vision says that public services librarians should offer, and administrators should support, the ability of the library to create information systems that make life easier for users. Two good examples are the Archie and Gopher systems on the Internet. The problem is that it was not librarians who invented these systems, but computer professionals.

Promote the design of information systems that require little or no learning time for effective use. Despite the fact that others have already inserted themselves into the information-organization game, as librarians we seem to be better than most at serving the user, guessing where the user may go wrong, and potentially in creating systems that will allow them to find what they need easily and quickly. Are we creating such systems? Not yet. Should we? I would say so. How? On an institutional basis, by collaborating with the "techies," the computer types, who want to create systems but are usually unable to discern the need to build systems that are easy to use. Look at Bitnet, at the Internet, at FTPing (file transferring) and telnetting; they could easily be made more user-friendly, and librarians should use their skills and service orientation to help the systems designers create better systems.

Correctly analyze users' questions and provide them with the information they need. This vision says that as a profession we haven't been performing, and we should raise our expectations of ourselves. It also implies our need to become expert on information in all formats—not just print.

Educate users to manage information. We return to the service orientation of libraries and librarians. But rather than waiting for the users to come to the desk and proclaim themselves ready for reference service, librarians need to go to them. And particularly in academic and special library environments, to go to them with a confidence that many librarians lack because they think that the faculty or the researchers or the lawyers are more knowledgeable or more powerful.

Initiate contact with potential information seekers to ensure a widespread understanding of professional services available to them, including assistance for those who do not wish to use the library independently. This folds two major issues into one vision. The first, of course, is similar to that of the librarian getting up and out of the library, seeking the initiative, "marketing," to use a term that some in our profession dislike. The second, and possibly even more important, point addresses the self-sufficiency argument once more. Since the visions group couldn't quite agree on whether users should be self-sufficient, those who did not care for user self-sufficiency compromised with the concept that users themselves should be able to request assistance if they wish.

Further the development of the virtual library, a concept of information housed electronically and deliverable without regard to its location or to time. This vision is also not a new vision, but it has hardly been implemented. As a profession, we speak these words, but we have not yet internalized them. As long as this is the case, other professions more imaginative and creative than ours will get there first; they may do a sloppy job of it, they may not provide ideal service, but they will provide the links, the means of getting at any kind of information anywhere. For example, librarians remain fettered to the concept that more information cannot be provided because we will have to charge some people, which will be inequitable. However, whether we provide the service or not, the inequity will occur, but that inequity will be done unto the information-seeking public by information providers other than libraries.

The implications for public services staff, all around, are tremendous and emphasize the arguments of those who say that the librarian of the future will have to be more sophisticated, better educated, and more professional. Take a look at what we are asking the public services librarian to do: make judgments about information, seek out users and educate them, create systems that are now being created by computer professionals, become psychologists to deduce who is capable of self-sufficient library use and who needs help, and move the boundaries of the library not only outside the walls of the building but so wide as to encompass the international nature of information. The location of information should not be an issue; the methods used to access information will become even more complex so that the body of knowledge and expertise that the public services librarian will require will go far beyond today's expectations.

And this will happen soon. In fact, it is already happening and is the cause of the increasing rumbles that we are hearing about lifelong education, certification or licensing, and other tools that enable librarians to remain up-to-date and be recognized as qualified.

Leadership Requirements

To look at leadership issues is to look at library administration. Everything that must be done in the future by the public services staff will have the imprimatur of the leader, the administrator.

The leadership category is intended to suggest the need for librarians to be proactive. If librarianship is to take responsibility for molding the information environment and ensuring that individuals receive the information they need to make knowledgeable decisions, we must be recognized as a force, a power that carries with it the weight of experience, expertise, and reasonableness. To that end, the visions statement suggests that we take steps to reinforce and emphasize our leadership role, which is now minimal or nonexistent. This is a courageous step; it will require boldness and some risk taking. Since we're not known for an excessive amount of either characteristic, the world will be surprised.

Take responsibility for information policy development, information technology application, environmental awareness, information research, and risk taking in making strategic choices in the information arena. That's a mouthful! It's pretty straightforward, though. Within the context of today's discussion, it says that public services librarians and administrators cannot sit back and allow the development of critical information policies and processes to be handed by default to others. No matter what kind or size of library you come from, you can broaden your conceptual framework from the limits of the library's walls outward. On a national level, there is some information policy development arising from the library world. An example is the *Principles of Public Information* document generated by NCLIS in 1990.

Under this vision, the item least obvious is that of environmental awareness. This does not refer to environment in the ecological sense; the intent is to say that we are responsible for a continuing awareness of the information environment in which we find ourselves so we can affect it appropriately and provide leadership to our users and profession. We have an awful tendency to say "Well, we're librarians. We are educated to organize, acquire, and access information. We're the best." However, it is possible that there are groups that are better information providers. We can't know this unless we are environmentally aware.

Accept accountability for the information services we provide. It is obvious what this means; it is not so obvious that there is agreement on how to do this or even whether it should be done. An important part of raising the expectations we have of ourselves includes accepting responsibility for our product. How will this affect public service librarians? Rather radically, I would suggest; it is a very different model from that of most reference desks.

*Identify and collaborate with strategic partners and allies in informa-
tion delivery.* Librarians must redefine themselves as they have been
redefining libraries for decades. One of the characteristics that has never
been significantly present in librarians as a group is a strong outreach to
the private sector, to those individuals and institutions that have the
resources that libraries do not have, and that are likely to want to invent
and market the services that we already know we can do well. The
successful professional of the future will be able to deal with partners, and
most particularly will be able to recognize the private sector as part friend
rather than part enemy. The librarian's public inability to negotiate, to
compromise, to make deals, hampers significantly the progress of our
libraries and underscores to nonlibrarians the characterization of the library
profession as stodgy and difficult.

Innovation Requirements

One would think that innovation, creativity, and risk taking would be taken
for granted as good things. That is not the case. Some librarians believe that
only a small percentage of us should be risk takers, because otherwise there
might be nobody at home to run the store. While this fear has some basis
in fact, what the profession really needs to aim toward is a situation in which
we have a large number of people who are simultaneously good leaders
(read "risk takers") and good managers (read "the library won't fall apart").[3]

*Experiment with new forms of organizational structure and staffing
within libraries to enable delivery of new types of services to users, especially
remote users or users of the growing "virtual library."* Librarians are
already experimenting with new forms of organizational structure, but
close examination reveals that the organization has not changed very much;
it has just acquired new names. Staffing, on the other hand, is significantly
different from what it was twenty or thirty years ago, and new types of
services are being introduced.

The visibility of the new services in those places willing to take the risk
of trying new things makes it seem as though the whole profession has
been catapulted into a new age. This is far from accurate; anyone really
scrutinizing the profession must look beyond the large research libraries,
and beyond the few pioneers, to recognize traditional services with a bit of
embellishment. As a profession, we are flirting with new services, but very
fearfully.

*Recognize and support the library without walls and the capacity of
library services to be provided in various environments.* A few university
libraries have created positions called "campus services librarians," or
similar titles. Within the university or corporate environment, we need to
go out to the users, rather than continuing to assume that the user will come

to us. When we successfully go out to the user, the user will understand that we are not rooted to our desks and chairs in the library and that we recognize our role in learning what their information needs are, on-site, and helping them without regard to the library as a building.

Recruitment and Development Requirements

The last issue is far from least. Many aspects of this topic worry us. We are troubled that so many library schools have closed, especially the ones that were located in prestigious research universities. We are alarmed about what this says about the way that academic administrators think of the library as an institution. We fret about the quality and nature of students graduating from library school, and the students themselves admit that for the most part they are anxious to seek security and are not willing to be risk-taking servers of the public. Much needs to be done in this area; the vision statement begins with just a few ideas.

Publicize the unique advantage at which the information age places librarians as information professionals. We do have a unique advantage; we are the only profession sufficiently expert to deal with the many issues being brought to bear by the changes rendered by technology. But what good does this advantage do us if no one else recognizes it? We have a massive need for a systematic approach to the rest of the world, to let them know that to be a librarian is to open doors to a fascinating career.

Strengthen the degree-granting programs, develop effective relationships with other information-related disciplines, and establish alternative modes for attaining professional credentials. The perceived weakness of our educational structure underlies many of the "vision" problems that disturb us today. The general lack of communication between the profession and the educators is not a new phenomenon but is hardly supportive of library schools as they come under attack by higher-education administrators. Attacking the problem in multiple ways is essential to: (1) enforce the link between library schools and libraries; (2) teach courses that have more intellectual substance than do the ones that are typically taught in a library school and, even more important, that are perceived as having more intellectual substance; (3) seriously examine the issue of licensing or certification of individuals as library professionals, in addition to or instead of accrediting library schools; and (4) remove the accreditation process from a personal-membership organization to which many librarians do not belong.

Attract and retain creative and innovative people. Most of us did not start out to be librarians. In fact, if you had told us when we were in high school that the career we would be engaged in for life was librarianship, most of us would have frowned in disbelief and turned up our noses. We entered the profession accidentally: we had a summer job in a library and it was fun; we needed a year to sort out career goals and spent that year working in a library; we couldn't get a job elsewhere and, after all, what could be a better job for English or history majors?

My sense is that this situation has not improved very much in the past twenty years. Libraries have constant contact with young people, in schools and in municipalities, and have failed to communicate to them the sense that this is an exciting profession. The buns and tennis shoes still exist; underscoring them is the constant complaining of the profession about salaries, about competition from the private sector, about free information with no recognition that information is not free.

We need to create out of librarianship a profession that is exclusive. That is, librarianship should be a profession that is competitive and difficult to enter, because the best and brightest are there. To achieve this vision will be no small feat; among the obstacles are our own self-image and our low-salary structure. Years, if not decades, will be required, but it is not only doable but necessary.

Incorporate different competencies and professionals into the emerging information-delivery environment. The evolving library, the one that we refer to as being without walls, will require more kinds of expertise than those gained in library school. Without defensiveness or a sense of inferiority, librarians must bring computer specialists, psychologists, and subject experts, among others, into the library, offering the library as an umbrella for a growing information nucleus for any organization. Most important, these people, whose degrees and training will be in areas other than librarianship, must be recognized, paid, and treated as well as people with an M.L.S. or a Ph.D. in librarianship. For some, this proposition goes against the grain. I suggest that it will be another trend that will be essential for our future survival.

Address the importance of continuing professional education. This point is an expansion of the earlier suggestions that library education requires strengthening, and that certification and licensing at the individual level are critical to achieve the vision of a profession that is at the center of the information age.

Conclusion

What does this all mean for public services librarians and administrators? The bottom line is that we have adopted, and continue to adopt, new information technologies, snapping up each new development eagerly. Now we need to remold our attitudes, our approach to our institutions and our constituencies, change our social values, to allow ourselves to be as forward looking and innovative as the tools that we provide access to and the information partners with whom we should be strategically allied.

Please think about the draft visions statement; determine whether it fits the future you would like to participate in. There's an increasing sense within the profession that this direction is essential for our future. It will happen best only if we all pursue the direction together.

Notes

1. Agnes M. Griffen, "Images of Libraries in Science Fiction," *Library Journal* 112 (Sept. 1, 1987): 137–42.

2. "Strategic Vision for Librarians," *CLR Reports* 6, no. 1 (Oct. 1992), 2. Note that the original form of the quoted portions of the vision statement has been changed here for editorial consistency.

3. John P. Kotter, *A Force for Change: How Leadership Differs from Management* (New York: Maxwell Macmillan International, 1990).

Implementation of Electronic Information Systems in Universities and the Implications for Change in Scholarly Research

Thomas Duncan

As someone from outside the library community, I was flattered to be asked to speak at this program, and I was intimidated by the breadth of the topic I was given. Within a general focus on how new technologies are changing the nature of publishing, scholarship, and communication, I was specifically charged to address the following questions:

- How will electronic publishing change the conduct of faculty research?
- What should faculty expect from electronic information systems as tools for research?
- What are the responsibilities of faculty members to develop and maintain scholarly electronic information systems?

To address these questions, I will review a variety of suggestions that have been presented in different forums. I will also outline some projects that are attempts to provide the data necessary to develop answers for these questions.

Ideas, Information, and Research

Ideas are the currency of the academy. The free exchange, open criticism, and independent exploration of ideas constitute basic activities of academics. The empirical data, sensory stimulations, philosophical inspirations, or other describable pathways to the formulation of ideas constitute both the record of and support for ideas. Our understanding of the world is based on a prevailing social and cultural climate of ideas, their interpretation, and acceptance of data or observations that support them or rejection of data or observations that conflict with them.

As Thomas Roszak noted in his 1986 book *The Cult of Information,* ideas create information.[1] The simple accumulation of facts does not become information unless ideas are presented within a context. We are surrounded by massive amounts of "information." We supposedly live in an "information society." However, many basic tools for academic study do not exist in electronic form. Information systems designed to accommodate the main ideas and patterns of study for most academic fields are only in the beginning stages of development.

A principal challenge for academics in the coming decade will be to design and implement disciplinewide information systems that facilitate the development of ideas. The development of such systems will require an environment where data and observations that support or refine ideas are easily accessible and available for critical examination and modification.

Academics currently spend enormous amounts of time trying to re-trieve from various sources empirical or philosophical bases for ideas that are connected to their research questions. As Alan B. Newman points out in a discussion about digital image databases, it seems that a better balance needs to be found between the contemplation of data and the retrieval of it.[2] The more effective our mechanisms for storage and retrieval of data, the more time and energy will be available to us to contemplate the significance of the data for the ideas that we are exploring. The recent and continuing enthusiasm for technology for electronic visualization provides an exam-ple. In the future, traditional definitions of literacy will need to be reexam-ined in light of an increasing understanding and use of information technology and electronic information systems as basic teaching tools.

To offer insight into this vision of the future, I first offer a review of recent suggestions concerning revised definitions of literacy in the context of the increasing use of information technology generally within society. I also will review the current state of the information technology infrastruc-ture within academia and the impact of information technology on the definition of literacy and the conduct of research. Finally, I will provide specific examples of current projects to develop the infrastructure.

A "New Literacy"

Traditional definitions of literacy derive from the technology of the printing press. The skills associated with reading and writing in one's own language are important to this definition. Some understanding of the cultural context in which you exist, its philosophical foundations and its connections to other cultures and philosophies, is also important. As B. M. Compaigne points out, the change in society to greater dependence on and use of information technology could potentially bring about a new concept of literacy.

Compaigne describes the process of change to a new literacy as consisting of two stages. The first stage is the simultaneous use of new processes and formats for substantive manipulation, retrieval, and storage, while the user is still thinking about the substance in traditional ways. Most academic information systems currently are at this stage.

The second stage requires a fundamental innovation in conceptualizing and processing information, a shift in perceptions about electronic information formats that is as fundamental as the shift was for traditional literacy to move from memory to written records.

Compaigne directs attention to a series of issues that will require study to develop this new concept of literacy. A new definition of literacy will include the ability to use electronic information systems to think holistically and intuitively rather than sequentially and logically. In his conception, faculty and institutions have the responsibility to address

- the underpinnings of traditional literacy and its relationship to current forces that impinge on literacy;
- the elements of information technology that shape future information processing;
- the correlation, if any, between available technology and the content in which users gather, create, store, and transmit information;
- the nontechnological factors that facilitate society's acceptance of elements of a literacy;
- the skills that make up a new literacy and how they complement or supplement traditional literacy skills.[3]

Other groups also have begun to address the need to reevaluate definitions of literacy. In 1987, the American Library Association appointed the Presidential Committee on Information Literacy. In their *Final Report*, issued in 1989, the committee defines information literacy as having the ability to "recognize when information is needed and . . . to locate, evaluate, and use effectively the needed information." The committee also points to the need for a reexamination of our current institutionalized notions of literacy. Specifically, the committee recommends that "we all must reconsider the ways we have organized information institutionally, structured information access, and defined information's role in our lives at home, in the community, and in the workplace."[4]

Pointing out that information technology challenges traditional notions of literacy will not, in fact, mean that definitions of literacy will change. For such changes to occur, academics and the institutions to which they belong must develop an understanding of the issue of literacy in an increasingly electronic world and the potential impact of revised definitions on educational practices.

Information Technology and the Conduct of Research

In 1989, a panel convened by the National Academy of Sciences, National Academy of Engineering, the Institute of Medicine, and the Committee on Science, Engineering, and Public Policy released a report, *Information Technology and the Conduct of Research*, that addresses the infrastructure necessary for the use of information technology in research.[5] The issues the panel addresses parallel those raised by Compaigne to reconsider the definition of literacy. This report examined present trends, future potential, and impediments to the use of information technology to support research from the viewpoint of the researcher who uses or will use this technology.

Overall, the panel suggested that information technology has led to improvements in research activities. Further opportunities will be presented as technology evolves. Widespread use of information technology has been hindered by a variety of financial, technical, institutional, and behavioral difficulties.

In particular, the panel addressed the current use of, and difficulties encountered in, data collection and analysis, communication and collaboration, and information storage and retrieval. For this discussion, I will focus on the latter two and outline the principal trends identified in the report.

The principal difficulty in collaboration and communication is incompatibility of networked systems and the use of software tools that are not powerful enough for the tasks at hand. The committee suggested a need for greater interoperability among networks and greater access to these networks and software tools that are designed to use these networks.

For information storage and retrieval, both factual and reference databases promise to be significant sources of knowledge for basic research. Factual databases present the following difficulties:

- They are difficult to access by researchers.
- They are difficult if not impossible to read.
- They are suspect with regard to data accuracy and validation.
- They are difficult if not impossible to merge with other data.

As a result, idiosyncratic methods for storing, organizing, and indexing data have been developed. One researcher's data essentially becomes inaccessible to most other researchers. For reference databases, most information searches currently are incomplete, cumbersome, inefficient, expensive, and executable only by specialists.

Underlying these difficulties, six impediments were identified: the costs of developing and maintaining databases; the lack of standards within and among disciplines; legal and ethical constraints surrounding data access; gaps in training and education of users of databases; risks of organizational change to develop or adopt databases; and the absence of an infrastructure for the use of information technology.

Scholarly Electronic Information Systems: Who Will Build the Information Technology Infrastructure?

I do not have the space here to discuss these six impediments in detail. I wish to focus on the infrastructure for scholarly information systems, which is thought by the panel to be the most important. To quote the panel:

> Just as use of a large collection of books is made possible by a building and shelves in which to put them, a cataloguing system, borrowing policies, and reference librarians to assist users, so the use of a collection of computers and computer networks is supported by the existence of institutions, services, policies, and experts—in short, by an infrastructure. On the whole, information technology is inadequately supported by current infrastructure.

The panel identified five elements necessary for an infrastructure for scholarly electronic information systems:

1. Access to experts who can help
2. Ways of supporting and rewarding those experts
3. Tools for developing software and a market in which the tools are evaluated against one another and disseminated
4. Communication links among researchers, experts, and the market
5. Analogs to the library to provide places where researchers can store and retrieve information

Little progress will be made until faculty and other academics assume a greater role in defining the functional requirements for this infrastructure and participate more fully in the development of it.

Faculty Responsibilities in an Electronic Academy

A prevailing stereotype of academic research is that of the independent scholar laboring on some issue where the search for "truth" or "knowledge" is independent of any connection to a larger social or cultural context. The purity of the quest for answers to questions or the development of ideas is strictly driven by the merit of the question or the novelty of the idea. In this sense, the data gathered are viewed as proprietary by the researcher.

Although drawn starkly, the ivory-tower academic is still very much a part of the academy. Traditional notions of literacy prevail, cybernetic intrusions are considered to be a technical exercise devoid of intellectual content, and the measure of "success" in such an environment is largely based on the quantity of publications and grant money generated.

To build an information technology infrastructure, academics at universities have a responsibility to participate in and foster the development of scholarly electronic information systems, foster collaboration with colleagues, and develop explicit practices that encourage sharing of data. These efforts can significantly enhance the building of and contribution to disciplinewide factual and reference databases.

In addition, faculty should simultaneously begin the reevaluation of

- traditional notions of research;
- traditional measures of scholarly activities;
- training of students who wish to enter the academy; and
- dissemination of academic work to satisfy a broader audience.

The changes that such reevaluation portends are as much a revolution within the academy as the building of the information technology infrastructure required to participate effectively in future research, teaching, and public service. The development of an effective information technology infrastructure and its impact will require serious attention by faculty.

Some Examples

Below I offer several examples of projects that attempt to address the construction of elements of an academic information technology infrastructure. These examples illustrate that the academic community is beginning to address the needed changes. The problem is vast and complicated. A single solution, a single technology, a single idea, will not guide development of an academywide infrastructure. The challenge is twofold: to construct elements of an infrastructure that are consistent with ideas, practices, and standards within disciplines, while encouraging and facilitating the sharing of common elements among disciplines. In addition, academics must recognize that the implementation of an academic information technology infrastructure will contain elements that are inconsistent with prevailing practices and will result in new and novel approaches to scholarly work.

The Human Genome Project

The Human Genome Project is an ambitious national project to decipher by the year 2005 the sequences for the fifty thousand to one hundred thousand genes that compose the human genome. Three national laboratories—Lawrence Livermore, Lawrence Berkeley, and Los Alamos—are coordinating the project. Seven academic centers at universities also have been set up. Potentially, hundreds of other laboratories will be set up.

In a recent article on the Human Genome Project in *Scientific American*, an account of the informatics (or information science) portion of this project provides useful insights.[6] Informatics staff describe their perception of their role in the project by saying "We don't fit in anywhere" or "You don't talk about this stuff at a general biology meeting; they'd think you were crazy." Despite the disdain they perceive, serious attention to informatics issues is indispensable to a project of this complexity. Informatics staff will be responsible for the development of every kind of computer support activity from data management and processing to DNA sequence analysis and the construction of genetic maps. The importance of informatics research and development for the Human Genome Project is reflected in the estimation that these activities will require as much as thirty percent of the budget for the Human Genome Project. These informatics activities require the implementation of the five elements needed for a more general academic information technology infrastructure. Yet the same behavioral and institutional constraints mentioned by the panel discussed above exist here.

The challenge to this project is to resolve an inherent conflict between the experimentalist culture of the academic biologist and the linear, logical culture of information technologists. The successes and failures in implementing an information technology infrastructure for the Human Genome Project will be instructive in the development of solutions for the larger academic community.

Educational Computing

Thus far, much of the extensive discussion about educational computing has focused on the technical aspects of teaching students how to use computer hardware and software. A more compelling theme is how to introduce students to the electronic information infrastructure envisioned for the future and how to train students to use the infrastructure to explore ideas and issues of interest to them.

A pair of recent articles in *EDUCOM Review* point to some directions of interest in this regard. N. Coombs discusses the impact of using high-speed networks to access electronic libraries and databases. As he sees the future, teachers "should focus more on helping students to know what questions to ask, where to find information, and how to structure the information once they have found it." Professors will profess less on the form of basic information in a discipline and focus more of their energies on acting as guides in the virtual cyberspace that will constitute the information infrastructure of their discipline.

As Coombs points out, this learning revolution will

> move the center of control from the teacher to the learner. People ferociously resist relinquishing power, and teachers are notoriously conservative about education. In the Middle Ages, professors read from their manuscripts to their classes. The printing press threatened that educational model. However, it was subsequently discovered that if students had the text available, teachers could expand on their texts and provide further explanations that enhanced learning. In a similar vein, many educators now fear that the computer will give students such powerful search and research engines that faculty will become redundant. Just as the printing press freed teaching to move to a higher level of conceptualization, so too will education in the information age transcend what has been common in our time. Good teachers will not be replaced by teaching assistants and teachers' aides, but they will be freed to define education in more exciting and creative terms.[7]

Regarding faculty participation in developing the educational component of an academic information infrastructure, in the other article R. J. Cavalier points out that the results of the time invested in educational computing run counter to the research paradigm for tenure and promotion. He states that the current paradigm for research as the predominant activity for academics inhibits the development of the educational information infrastructure that is needed to parallel the research information infrastructure described by the panel report.

Cavalier argues that teaching should be put on a level with research in the evaluation of faculty for promotion and tenure. Furthermore, the definition of teaching should be broadened to include the development of the educational information infrastructure, including the development of educational software and computing technology.[8]

The National Research and Education Network (NREN)

The NREN is a national effort to interconnect members of the nation's education and research community at gigabit-per-second data-transmission rates, thereby facilitating research, communications, and education.[9] Over the last decade, the development of NSFNet, the precursor of the NREN, has been a significant factor in facilitating communications among researchers around the country.

With the development of the NREN, the critical telecommunications component of an academic information technology infrastructure will be enhanced and universally available to faculty, staff, and students in universities. Ultimately it will be available in elementary and secondary schools. The extent to which wide availability of networks will affect precollege educational practices is not yet known. However, the predictions are that the availability of wide-area networks combined with well-designed, easy-to-use information resources will significantly change our educational system.

The Museum Informatics Project (MIP)

The Museum Informatics Project is an effort by the University of California at Berkeley to coordinate the application of information technology in museums and other organized, nonbook collections. This effort is an example of how components of an academic information infrastructure will be built within a research university. The materials housed in these collections are significant and fundamental research and teaching resources. For many areas of study, these materials represent the only sources of primary data upon which these fields are built.

The collections of a research university like Berkeley are vast, administratively fragmented, and frequently underfunded even for basic operations. Such a situation is not unique to Berkeley. Rather, such situations seem to be the norm within academia, despite the importance of these collections for research, teaching, and public service.

The challenges to this project are not only to implement the elements of a scholarly electronic information infrastructure, but also to develop a working environment where faculty, staff, and students in disciplines that have previously had little or no connection to one another can interact to develop solutions to their mutual and often overlapping needs for information technology.

Although academics working with a few collections have a great deal of experience working with databases, there is much to be done to develop the data models, functional requirements, and networked systems that will facilitate the use of these collections in a distributed, networked computing environment. A project like MIP has the possibility to open new avenues of teaching and research, make more widely available the unparalleled collections that have traditionally only been available to a few researchers, and to offer to the wider public the opportunity to explore the primary materials associated with academic study.

Summary

Information technology will change the nature of academic work. Exactly what those changes are to be is yet to be known. The ideas I offer here suggest that much research needs to be done on the design and implementation of the basic information technology infrastructure for the electronic academy. As this infrastructure is designed, the technology also challenges traditional concepts of literacy, data ownership, faculty criteria for productivity, presentation of results, and teaching techniques. The solutions to these complicated and challenging issues portend an exciting future in which an increasing integration of information technology within universities will produce an increasingly electronic academy. To all who wish to participate, the task is exciting in its scope and fundamental in its implications.

Notes

1. Thomas Roszak, *The Cult of Information: The Folklore of Computing and the True Art of Thinking* (New York: Pantheon, 1986), 238.

2. Alan B. Newman, "Present at the Revolution," *Museum News,* Jan.–Feb. 1992, 53–56.

3. B. M. Compaigne, "Information Technology and Cultural Change: Toward a New Literacy," in *Issues in New Information Technology* (Norwood, N.J.: Ablex, 1988), 145–78.

4. American Library Association, Presidential Committee on Information Literacy, *Final Report* (Chicago: American Library Assn., 1989).

5. Panel on Information Technology and the Conduct of Research, *Information Technology and the Conduct of Research: The User's View* (1989).

6. D. Erickson, "Hacking the Genome," *Scientific American* 266, no. 4 (1992): 128–37.

7. N. Coombs, "Teaching in the Information Age," *EDUCOM Review* 27, no. 2 (1992): 32–37.

8. R. J. Cavalier, "Shifting Paradigms in Higher Education and Educational Computing," *EDUCOM Review* 27, no. 3 (1992): 32–35.

9. R. Aiken and others, *National Science Foundation Implementation for Interagency Interim NREN* (National Science Foundation, 1992). This is a thirty-one-page PostScript manuscript available by anonymous FTP from the National Science Foundation.

About the Speakers

Dr. Thomas Duncan is a faculty assistant for the Museum Informatics Project and an associate professor of integrative biology at the University of California at Berkeley. The Museum Informatics Project is working with various collections on the University of California campus to develop a state-of-the art museum electronic information system. A coalition of campus museums is providing a testing ground for systems development and operations.

Peter S. Graham is an associate university librarian for technical and networked services at Rutgers–The State University of New Jersey. For three years he was also an associate vice-president for information services, responsible for Rutgers' central and systemwide academic and administrative computing facilities. He was a librarian at Columbia University and Indiana University during the early days of the Research Libraries Group. Graham studied at Columbia while working as a systems manager and did graduate work in English Renaissance literature at Columbia and at Oxford University. He earned his M.L.S. at Indiana University. A distinguished speaker and writer, Graham has been a regular contributor to discussions in our profession about the directions that we ought to be taking as the electronic future looms upon us.

Arnold Hirshon has been the university librarian at Wright State University since 1990. Prior to his current position, Hirshon was the associate director of university library services at Virginia Commonwealth University, and he held professional positions at Duke University and Wayne State University. He received his M.L.S. from Indiana University and a master's degree in public administration from Wayne State University. During 1991–92, Hirshon served as the president of the Association for Library Collections & Technical Services, and he has served the association in many other capacities, including four years as the chair of the Budget and Finance Committee and six years as editor of the *RTSD Newsletter*. His substantial publication record includes writings on acquisitions, library technology, organizational planning, and cataloging.

Dr. Susan K. Martin is the university librarian at Georgetown University. Previously she served as university librarian at Johns Hopkins University, and prior to that time she worked as a systems librarian at Harvard and at the University of California at Berkeley. Library automation and networking have been the focus of most her books and articles. During her career, she has been a consultant for numerous libraries and companies, working in library management and technology.

Theodor (Ted) Holm Nelson has had a long and distinguished career in the information industry. Nelson coined both the term and the concept of hypertext more than twenty-five years ago. Today he is actively engaged in Project Xanadu, a developmental project that seeks to create a worldwide publishing network based on a radical server program for free-structured and interconnected documents. One aspect of Xanadu is to create a program to provide information providers with a royalty-publishing network. Nelson received his B.A. from Swarthmore College and holds a master's degree in social relations from Harvard. He has been a distinguished fellow at AutoDesk, Inc., and a visiting professor of information science at the University of Strathclyde in Glasgow, Scotland. He is the author of the books *Computer Lib* and *Literary Machines.* His autobiography, *My Computer Life,* and his *Biostrategy and Polymind* are scheduled for publication in the near future.